A D

GROOMING YOUR DOG

A practical step-by-step program for maintaining and improving your dog's appearance.

Tetra⊙Press

No. 16021

A DOG OWNER'S GUIDE TO

GROOMING YOUR DOG

A practical step-by-step program for maintaining and improving your dog's appearance.

Suzanne Ruiz

A Salamander Book

© 1987 Salamander Books Ltd
Published by Tetra Press, 201 Tabor Road, Morris Plains, NJ 07950

ISBN 3-923880-66-9

Library of Congress number: 87-050048

All correspondence concerning the content of this volume should be addressed to Tetra Press.

Contents

Credits

Editor: Jo Finnis
Designer: Philip Gorton
Photographs: Luis Ruiz; Marc Henrie – front cover; title page; 15, 17, 35 (top), 41, rear endpaper
Illustrations: Ray Hutchins
Color origination: Rodney Howe Ltd
Typesetting: AKM Associates (UK) Ltd
Printed in Portugal

Author

Suzanne is a qualified Dog Beautician and has, for many years, run the leading open-plan grooming parlour in Sussex, England. In the parlour, she uses the very latest equipment and techniques.
Suzanne has been grooming for 15 years. She taught herself initially, grooming her friends' pets, and found such a demand for her services that she bought a salon.
Runner-up twice for Groomer of the Year in the UK, she won this coveted award in 1984. At the beginning of 1986, Suzanne was appointed Examiner of the City and Guilds Certificate in Grooming.
Suzanne has also been breeding and showing dogs for 25 years. She breeds and judges Bichon Frisés, and breeds and shows Chihuahuas.

Photographer

Luis Ruiz is a semi-professional photographer, who began his working life in the hotel and catering business.
Before settling in England with his wife, Suzanne, Luis worked at the famous Minzah Hotel in Marrakech, frequented by the rich, royal and famous – Elizabeth Taylor, the King of Spain and Charles Laughton.
When he moved to England, Luis became Manager of the world famous restaurant, The Mascot, in Brighton, later moving to the Eaton.
Photography having always been his fervent hobby, Luis has recently devoted more time to his photographic career, and has won some highly-respected awards for his work.
Luis has teamed up with his wife at the grooming parlour to photograph Suzanne in action.

US consultant

Shirlee Kalstone is the author of eight books and numerous articles on the grooming and care of dogs and cats. She has received several awards from the Dog Writers' Association of America.
Shirlee has written the regular monthly grooming column for *Pure-Bred Dogs*, the *American Kennel Club Gazette*, for several years. She is also the organizer of Intergroom, an international educational conference for groomers.

Author's acknowledgment

The author would like to thank Pam Nicholls for all her help and advice in putting the book together.

Introduction

Your responsibilities

Grooming is a vital aspect of dog and puppy care and you, as a dog owner, must undertake responsibility for your pet in this respect as well as any other, such as feeding, housing and regular veterinary checks. It is not just a matter of regular brushing and combing – on a daily basis with long-haired dogs – but includes care of eyes, ears, teeth, nails and anal glands, as well as treating external parasites.

Some breeds also require periodic scissoring, clipping or handstripping, factors which need careful consideration before choosing your dog (see Chapter One). Many dog owners are unable or unwilling to make regular visits to a canine beautician or dog grooming salon. This book presents detailed instructions and accompanying photographs and illustrations for every aspect of grooming your dog in your own home environment.

Professional grooming

The book has not been conceived as an instruction manual for the aspiring professional groomer, although having mastered the basic techniques presented here, some of you may be encouraged to develop your interest further. You may then wish to embark on a training course in professional grooming.

Show grooming

I have not attempted to cover the specialist task of grooming for the show ring. For many breeds, this involves complex grooming techniques, only perfected through years of experience.

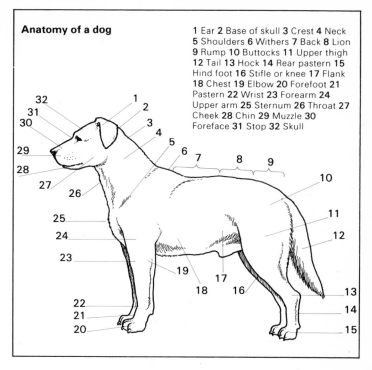

Anatomy of a dog

1 Ear 2 Base of skull 3 Crest 4 Neck 5 Shoulders 6 Withers 7 Back 8 Lion 9 Rump 10 Buttocks 11 Upper thigh 12 Tail 13 Hock 14 Rear pastern 15 Hind foot 16 Stifle or knee 17 Flank 18 Chest 19 Elbow 20 Forefoot 21 Pastern 22 Wrist 23 Forearm 24 Upper arm 25 Sternum 26 Throat 27 Cheek 28 Chin 29 Muzzle 30 Foreface 31 Stop 32 Skull

Above left: *Suzanne Ruiz with her own dog. Grooming can be enjoyable as well as rewarding – for you and your dog!*

Above: *This terminology is used within the book, so begin by getting to know those terms as yet unfamiliar to you.*

The book plan

The book is divided into two main sections. **Section One** presents the fundamentals of dog grooming – the basic equipment you require; brushing and combing techniques; scissoring; clipping; bathing; drying; care of eyes, ears, teeth, nails, anal glands; external parasites and their treatment.

   Section Two focuses on the main coat types that require extensive grooming: silky, straight; woolly, curly; harsh with undercoat; Terrier/Spaniel handstrip coats, including alternative methods of grooming – handstripped or clipped/scissored (see Chapter One regarding Spaniels and Terriers). Step-by-step instructions and accompanying photographs are set out for the popular breeds within each coat category, carefully and explicitly guiding you through every stage of the grooming process from beginning to end.

The rewards

There is a great deal of enjoyment to be gained in mastering the art of grooming your own dog, and tremendous satisfaction in winning the admiration of people when they see the result of your labours. To have a healthy, clean and smart-looking canine companion is a constant pleasure.

Section One

GROOMING EQUIPMENT AND TECHNIQUES

Chapter One

CHOOSING YOUR DOG

When buying a dog, there are many factors which you need to take into consideration. Obviously, it is not merely a case of choosing the dog which you find the most appealing; you must take into account its size, the amount of exercise and food it requires, and make a choice in accordance with your lifestyle.

A major consideration, which many people overlook, is the care that the dog's coat demands. All dogs require regular brushing and combing, as well as care of nails, teeth, ears and eyes. But a short-haired breed, such as a Whippet or Bulldog, will require the minimum of grooming, whereas long-haired breeds need constant, daily coat care using various techniques depending on the length and type of coat.

Ask the breeder

I feel it is very important that breeders explain to prospective buyers the care that the dog will need, including grooming requirements. Unfortunately, some breeders fail to do this, which can often result in owners neglecting their dogs' coats. As well as looking unkempt and unattractive, the ungroomed dog will fall prey to troublesome parasites and skin problems, and the only solution may be to strip the coat right down to the skin (see Chapter Three on The

Above right: *Poodles require daily coat care in addition to a six to eight-weekly clip to keep them looking attractive.*

Right: *The Dalmation is a smooth-coated breed requiring minimum coat care. Grooming twice-weekly only is needed.*

Neglected Coat). You, as the new owner, must accept the responsibility for your pet's welfare from the time you make your choice. Before departing with your new dog, talk to the breeder about grooming, and gain the benefit of his or her experience with the breed.

Spaniels and Terriers

I would like to mention here that, in theory, all Spaniels and Terriers should be handstripped, and I have explained this technique in detail in Section Two. However, I have also included an alternative, clipped method. The method you choose should be dictated by the texture and quality of the dog's coat, the dog's tolerance level and the amount of time and energy you can spare for the task. Handstripping takes several hours to complete, which will be both demanding of you and your dog, but the end result is a natural look typical of the breed.

Clipping may be preferable for many owners, since it is less time-consuming and easier to manage. By clipping a 'handstrip' coat, the hair will become softer and the colour of the coat paler.

Grooming requirements across the breeds
The chart below gives an indication of the amount and complexity of grooming required for each breed of dog, categorized as follows:

Minimum coat care Dogs in this category are generally short or smooth-coated breeds. They will normally require twice-weekly grooming of the coat. This should be carried out more frequently during times of natural moult of the coat, or when the temperature changes induce excessive hair loss.

Nails, ears, eyes and anal glands should be checked at the same time as grooming the coat.

Bathing of these breeds of dog

Grooming chart for all breeds

Minimum grooming
Affenpinscher; American Staffordshire Terrier; Australian Cattle Dog; Basenji; Basset Hound; Beagle; Black and Tan Coonhound; Boston Terrier; Boxer; Bull Terrier; Bullmastiff; Chihuahua; Dachshund; Dalmation; Doberman; Elkhound; English Toy Terrier; French Bulldog; Great Dane; Greyhound; Jack Russell Terrier; Pointer; Rhodesian Ridgeback; Staffordshire Bull Terrier; Weimaraner; Whippet

Equipment
Nail clippers
Bristle brush
Hound glove
Chamois leather
Coat dressing (optional)

Daily grooming
Afghan Hound; Akita; Bearded Collie; Bernese Mountain Dog; Bloodhound; Border Collie; Borzoi; Briard; Brittany Spaniel; Cairn Terrier; Cavalier King Charles Spaniel; Chow Chow; Clumber Spaniel; Corgi; Deerhound; English Springer Spaniel; German Shepherd Dog; Irish Wolfhound; King Charles Spaniel; Labrador Retriever; Lhasa Apso; Maltese Terrier; Newfoundland; Old English Sheepdog; Papillon; Pekingese; Pomeranian; Pug; Pyrenean Mountain Dog; Retrievers; Rottweiler; St Bernard; Saluki; Samoyed; Setters; Scottish Terrier; Shetland Sheepdog; Shih Tzu; Smooth Fox Terrier; Tibetan Spaniel; Tibetan Terrier; Welsh Springer Spaniel; Yorkshire Terrier

Equipment
Nail clippers
Bristle brush
Pin brush
Slicker brush
Comb
Hound glove
Scissors
Electric clippers (for groin and feet)
Blade Nos 10, 15
Coat dressing (optional)
Ribbon (optional)

Additional grooming
Airedale; American Cocker Spaniel; American Water Spaniel; Bedlington Terrier; Bichon Frisé; Border Terrier; Dandie Dinmont Terrier; English Cocker Spaniel; Griffon; Irish Terrier; Irish Water Spaniel; Kerry Blue Terrier; Lakeland Terrier; Maltese Terrier (scissored); Old English Sheepdog (scissored); Poodle; Schnauzer; Welsh Springer Spaniel; Welsh Terrier; West Highland White Terrier; Wire Fox Terrier; Yorkshire Terrier (scissored)

Equipment
Nail clippers
Pin brush
Slicker brush
Comb
Scissors
Thinning scissors
Electric clippers
Blade Nos 7f, 10, 15
Stripping knife
Ribbon/bows

only needs to be carried out when they begin to smell 'doggy'.

Daily coat care Breeds of dog in this category require daily brushing and combing to remove all the dead undercoat and to prevent matting or felting. The feet and pads should be checked for foreign bodies, such as grass seeds between the toes. Particular attention should be paid to the featherings (the long hair on the legs, ears and tail), belly and face, which require a thorough combing to prevent tangling.

Nails, ears and eyes can be checked as part of the daily grooming session, or at least twice-weekly. Bathe every 3–12 months according to your preference and circumstances.

Note that where a smooth-coated breed appears in this category, its inclusion is due to particular daily grooming requirements in addition to the minimum coat care, eg nose wrinkles or pendulous ears, such as in the case of the Bloodhound, Pogs and Pekes; excessive facial wrinkles require daily cleansing.

Additional grooming These breeds of dog require daily coat care as above, plus a six to eight-weekly clip, strip or scissoring, depending on the breed and the owner's preference. The dogs in this category will be bathed prior to scissoring or clipping as a matter of course; handstripped dogs are bathed **after** stripping.

Below: *Although the Bloodhound is smooth-coated, its facial wrinkles need daily cleansing with water and cotton wool.*

Chapter Two

THE BASIC GROOMING KIT

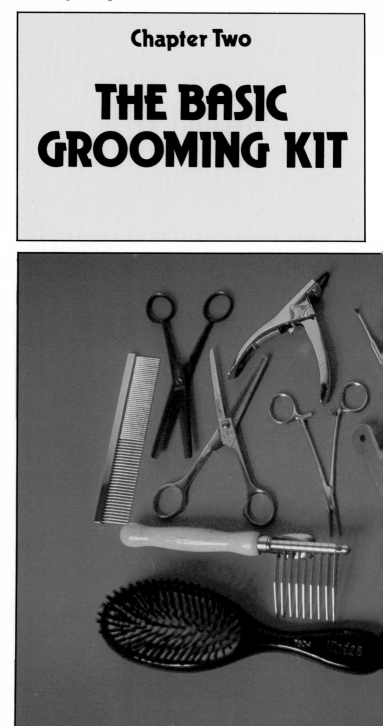

The list of equipment below will be sufficient to meet the grooming needs of any breed of dog. Obviously, there will be some variation in what is required for certain breeds: short or smooth-coated dogs will only require a bristle brush and a hound glove; obviously only handstrip coats will require a stripping knife (see Section Two for specific equipment required for each coat-type/breed).

Brushes

Pin brush This is most suitable for regular brushing of long-coated breeds such as the Afghan, Pekingese and Saluki.

Slicker brush This is a light-weight brush recommended for use on curly coats such as the Poodle.

Below: *Clockwise from far left: half fine/half coarse comb; double-serrated thinning scissors; single-serrated thinning scissors; guillotine nail clippers; artery forceps; dental scaler; slicker brush; hound glove; pin brush; stripping knife; bristle brush; de-matting comb.*

Bristle brush This has tufts of soft, pure bristles, best for straight, silky-haired breeds such as the Yorkshire Terrier.

Hound glove This is suitable for use on smooth-coated dogs such as the Great Dane, Chihuahua and members of the Hound family generally.

Combs
Half fine/half coarse comb This is the best type of comb for general use: a long, metal comb consisting of half fine and half coarse teeth.

De-matting comb This has long, widely-spaced teeth with a handle specifically designed to deal with badly-matted coats.

7" barber scissors These scissors have long, straight blades that taper to a point. I recommend a pair of scissors with seven-inch blades for general use, preferably with a finger rest, but they are available in various lengths to suit your preference or purpose.

Thinning scissors These are used for thinning out the coat and blending rather than for heavy cutting. I would recommend the type with one serrated blade and one regular scissor blade.

Clippers
Oster clippers are probably the best-known and best quality electric clippers available. There are various models – for amateur and professional use – to choose from. Your local grooming equipment supplier will be able to help you to select one best suited to your individual needs.

Oster Small Animal Clippers A5 and A2 These two models are used by professional groomers. The *A5* has detachable blades of different sizes to achieve different cutting lengths and effects, while the *A2* has a detachable cutter-head. The *A5*

Below: *These clippers* (Oster 134 Mark II) *are suitable for home use. The three most useful blades are Coarse, Medium and Fine.*

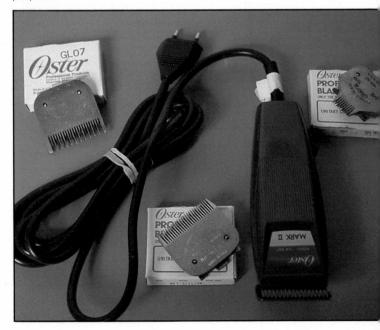

Clipper blade chart

Professional clippers	Pet clippers	Cutting action
No 5	Coarse	Plucking length. Leaves hair ⅝-¾in (16-19mm) long. For all over clipping.
No 7f	—	Semi-plucking length. Leaves hair ¼in (6mm) long. Good for Spaniels.
No 10	Medium	Medium length. For general and underbody clipping.
No 15	Fine	Medium to close cutting. For use on the feet of Poodles.

is the popular choice for professionals because of the ease in changing the blades.

Smaller models and pet clippers

These are more limited in their adjustability than the *A5* or *A2* models but are quite adequate for private use.

Below: *Two types of de-matting comb with widely-spaced teeth. Use these with caution to remove small knots and tangles.*

Clipper blades

For the professional clippers, there are a wide variety of blades available, ranging from No 4 to No 40. The No 4 blade has the widest spaced teeth, leaving the hair ⅝-¾in (16-19mm) long; the No 40 has the closest set teeth for extra-fine cutting. To achieve the trims illustrated in Section Two, I have used just four blades from the Oster range: Nos 5, 10, 15 and 7f, the most the pet owner is ever likely to need. With the smaller Oster models, the

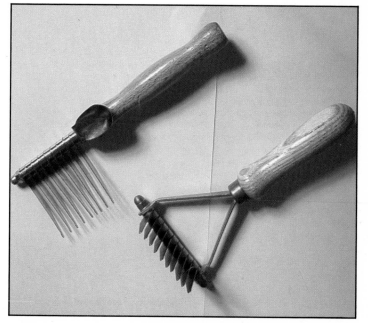

equivalent blades would be a Skip Tooth, Coarse, Medium and Fine (see chart).

Clipper and blade care

Both blades and clippers must be cleaned after use. Remove all loose hair and apply the blade wash recommended by the manufacturers to the blades. Oil the clippers occasionally, again following the manufacturers' instructions carefully. The blades will need to be regularly sharpened and the clippers serviced, both depending on frequency of use.

Stripping knives

Although there are many different styles of stripping knife, they generally consist of a blade with sharp teeth giving a cutting action, mounted in a handle made of wood, plastic or aluminium. Different sizes of teeth give varying degrees of fineness. Both left-handed and right-handed knives are available. Experimentation is the only way to find which knife suits your purposes best.

Nail clippers

There are a variety of nail clippers available, but I would strongly recommend using the guillotine type, rather than the plier type. The latter squeezes the dog's nail, causing it aggravation.

Ear forceps

These can be either curved or straight and are used for removing unwanted hair from the dog's ears which cannot be reached by the fingers.

Dental scaler

To remove tartar from your dog's teeth. However, I do recommend that this task is best done by your veterinarian.

Dryers

There are many types of dryers available for private and professional use. Although a hand-held, human hair dryer is perfectly adequate for the owner to use on his or her pet, a professional canine power dryer is quicker and easier to use.

Professional cabinet dryer. This is the type of dryer used in professional grooming salons, in which two to six dogs can be dried at the same time.

Cage dryer This dryer can be attached to a travelling box or cage, into which the warm air is blown, thus saving a lot of hard work.

Floor or stand dryers These professional power dryers are mounted on a strong stand, adjustable in height, allowing the use of both hands during the drying process. These dryers vary in size and power.

Grooming tables

There is a range available. A

sturdy table with a non-slip, rubber top which can be folded up and stored away, or transported, is the most useful.

Professional groomers mostly use electrically operated tables which can be raised, lowered or revolved, to cater for all sizes and shapes of dog.

Restrainer

This adjustable clamp can be fixed on to the side of the grooming table. It has a loop that can be put round the dog's neck to hold it in place. A restrainer is a useful aid to keeping your dog steady while you work, and vital if you should leave it unattended.

Left: *This small power dryer has been mounted on a stand enabling the groomer to use both hands for brushing and holding.*

Below: *A collapsible grooming table is useful. Never leave your dog unattended on the table. If you have to, use a restrainer.*

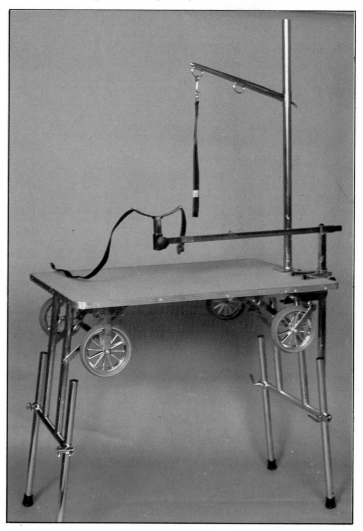

Chapter Three

BASIC GROOMING TECHNIQUES

BRUSHING AND COMBING

Of the many brushes available, consider the slicker brush to be the most versatile for the pet dog owner. Sympathetically used, ie with a light touch, it can be effective on all but the smooth-coated breeds. It is excellent for removing dead coat and will cope efficiently with burrs, seeds, dried mud and one hundred and one other adherents that the active dog's coat is likely to attract.

When using the slicker brush, hold it lightly and ensure that the metal teeth do not dig into the dog's skin. Part the coat and brush each layer, paying special attention to the areas most likely to mat, ie ears, chest, the inside of the elbows, tail, trousers, stomach and between the toes.

After brushing through the entire coat, take the 'comb test'. Will the comb glide easily through all the above-mentioned areas without meeting resistance? If the answer is yes, congratulations!

Below: *Pay special attention to the 'underarm' hair to prevent matting. Do not hold the legs at an unnatural angle to the body.*

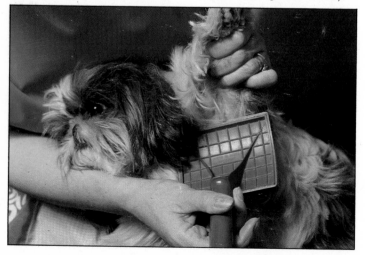

Toy breeds
Owners of toy breeds often prefer to use a bristle brush or pin brush on their pets. The same principle applies, but on small dogs the legs and stomachs are particularly vulnerable to matting.

Smooth coats
The dual purpose hound glove is excellent for the smooth-coated dog. It has thick, short bristles on one side to remove loose hair,

Above: *Beards should be brushed thoroughly where food collects. It is kinder to brush downwards and towards the body.*

and rubberised studs on the reverse to massage the skin. A wipe over with a chamois leather or silk scarf will give the finishing touch.

Puppy grooming
Give your new puppy a day or two to settle down and then begin a routine which will stand both you and the dog in good stead always.

Select a grooming area away

Below: *The comb test. If your brushing of the coat has been thorough, the comb will glide with ease through the hair.*

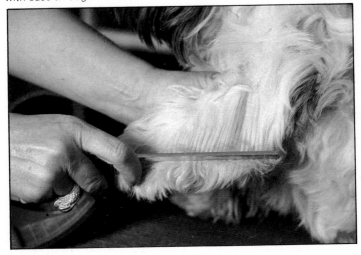

from noise and distractions. Place a towel or rubber mat on a solid working surface, preferably a table, and stand the puppy on it. Holding it gently but firmly, brush it all over using light, almost stroking movements. This will familiarize the dog with the brush and will teach it to submit to your handling.

Then examine the puppy's ears, look at its teeth, pick up each paw and check the nails (see Chapter Six). Talk to the puppy reassuringly and give it lots of praise. If the puppy attempts to bite the brush, and it probably will, discourage this immediately with a firm 'no'. The ten-week-old puppy that playfully growls at you and snatches at the brush may be appealing, but allow this habit to go unchecked and the same dog at ten months may prove impossible to groom.

Little and often should be the maxim. Five minutes daily should suffice for a three-month-old puppy, and this can be extended, depending on the breed and its requirements, as the dog matures. Immediately the grooming session is over, take the puppy down from the table or bench and give it lots of praise.

Below: *It is safest to groom a small puppy while holding it firmly in your lap. While you groom, talk to it reassuringly.*

The neglected coat

Hopefully, if you have followed the suggestions in 'Early Days', your adult dog will enjoy its grooming sessions, and its coat, as a result, will be healthy, shiny and totally free of tangles.

It may be however, for varying circumstances, that your dog's grooming sessions have been missed, with the result that some or all of the following areas of your dog's coat are matted: moustache, ears, trousers, chest, elbows and tummy. In severe cases of neglect, where removal of dead hair has been totally ignored and grooming has been neglected altogether, it may be necessary for the coat to be completely sheared off using clippers. This must be done by a veterinarian or a professional groomer. Once the coat is off, careful daily grooming can then be undertaken.

If only parts of the coat are matted, it is possible, if the owner is patient and the dog of equable temperament, for the coat to be saved. Densely matted areas can be split through with scissors. The scissors must be held with the blades pointing downwards, eliminating the possibility of the skin being nicked. An oil-based conditioner or a tangle-removing product can be applied, or a little cornflour rubbed into the coat. Make sure the mats are saturated

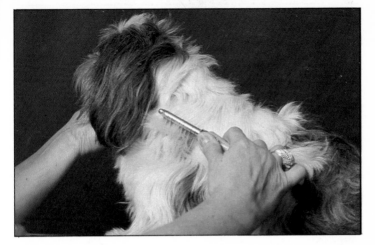

with the preparation, using your fingers to work it into the hair. Leave the conditioner on the coat until the hair is almost dry. Then, use your fingers to gently but persistently pull the mats apart into smaller clumps of hair and use a wide-toothed comb to free the tangles. In this way, the dog's coat can be carefully restored to a manageable state. This work may have to be done over a period of several days, if the dog and owner are not to become fractious.

Once the major knots are dealt

Above: *When using a de-matting comb, insert the comb into the mat and gently pull downwards. Never pull upwards.*

with, the dog can be bathed and a liberal application of conditioner applied to the affected areas. Bathing should not be undertaken before de-matting, since water tends to tighten the mats making them impossible to remove. Leave the conditioner on for a few minutes and then rinse off very thoroughly. However, this does not apply to everyday small tangles, which should be tackled wet. Any remaining, minor mats should be tackled with the slicker brush as the dog is being dried.

Below: *This badly matted hair has been clipped away from a severely neglected coat. Do not attempt this yourself.*

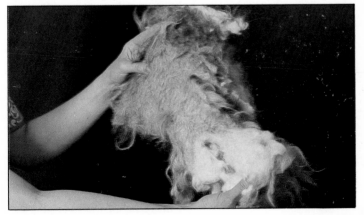

27

CLIPPING

How to hold
Hold the clippers in the correct position (see photograph), ie like holding a pencil. When using the clippers, it is important to keep your wrist flexible – if your dog should suddenly move, you could nick the skin, or at least clip hair from the wrong place.

Technique
Make sure the blade is flat against the surface you are clipping – do not dig the clippers into the skin. Special care must be taken when clipping around the head, face, feet, tail and stomach. As a general rule, clip with the lay of the coat unless otherwise instructed, a notable exception being the Poodle's face (see Section Two, pages 64-75). Never rush your clipper work; feed the hair slowly into the blade.

Clipper burn
Clipper burn is a painful rash where the dog's skin becomes red and irritated, which can develop into open sores with persistent scratching. It can be caused by allowing the clipper blade to become too hot, or by close clipping of the sensitive areas: the face, throat, underside of tail, stomach or genitals. Avoid this occurring by testing the blade against your wrist, and if it is too hot to touch, spray with a coolant specifically designed for this purpose.

To prevent irritation, you can buy an 'after-clip' preparation for use on the sensitive areas after clipping. White dogs tend to have more sensitive skin than darker-coloured dogs.

Visit your veterinarian if sores develop from the clipper rash.

SCISSORING

Scissoring is the most difficult aspect of grooming and it can take years of practice to perfect the technique. If you achieve a good result, it can also be the most rewarding part of grooming your own dog.

How to hold
The correct way to hold a pair of scissors is to place the thumb in the largest hole and the third finger in the smaller hole, moving only the thumb up and down.

Technique
Practise your cutting action on a piece of sheepskin. Aim for a level, plush finish. Do not press the scissors into the coat, but lay them flat just on the surface, cutting very little at a time as you move over the area to be cut. When the blades are held flat against the hair ends, the shafts are cut as wide as the root and look thick and profuse. With the blades held at an angle, the hair ends are narrowed and weakened.

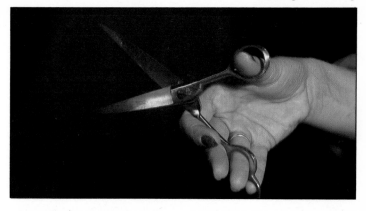

Above: *Scissoring is the most difficult part of grooming. Hold the scissors as shown, and use held flat against the hair.*

Below: *This is the correct way to hold clippers, to balance them in your hand. Follow the lay of the coat, except on the head.*

Below left: *Make sure the blade is kept flat against the surface you are clipping. Feed the hair slowly into the clipper.*

Below: *Do not dig into the skin with the blade. Keep your wrist flexible to avoid hurting the dog if it moves suddenly.*

Chapter Four

BATHING

Equipment
Large sink or bath; Spray hose; Rubber mat; Good quality dog shampoo; Conditioner; Sponge; Cotton wool; Towels; Plastic-toothed brush; Plastic apron

Shampoos
There is a whole range of shampoos, formulated and PH-balanced for dogs:

All-purpose These are suitable for all coat textures and colours, some with additional conditioning agents to add lustre or to restore damaged hair.
Tearless or baby shampoo A mild shampoo for use on the head. Use a puppy shampoo for puppies.
Colour These are formulated to enhance various coat colours. They are not permanent dyes.
Medicated These are designed for dogs with itchy or flaky skins, or suffering from non-specific forms of Dermatitis.
Insecticidal These are specially designed to kill fleas and ticks. Make sure you follow the manufacturers' instructions.

How often?
Generally speaking, a dog does not need to be bathed too frequently. Obviously, if your dog rolls in dirt, which many dogs seem to enjoy, it will have to be washed. When a long-coated dog starts to smell 'doggy', give daily attention to the anal area where faeces may adhere to the coat. Dogs that are clipped, stripped or scissored every six to eight weeks will be bathed beforehand (see Section Two),

but many Terriers and short-haired dogs can go up to six months or more without needing a bath. It depends entirely on their lifestyle and their owners' attitude.

There is a school of thought which suggests that if a dog is bathed too often, natural oils are stripped from the coat. However, with modern shampoos and conditioners, this should not happen and the owner must not be afraid to bath the dog when it is thought necessary.

Bathing procedure
Prepare your equipment before putting the dog in the bath or sink. It is a good idea to wear protective clothing, or you may get a bath too! Place the dog in the bath or sink on top of the rubber mat – you may need someone's help if your dog is a large and heavy one. Put a little cotton wool into each ear to prevent any water entering the ear canal, which could lead to

Above right: *Avoiding eyes, wet the dog all over with warm water from the spray hose, taking great care to avoid the dog's eyes.*

Right: *By holding the dog's head upwards a little, as shown here, you will help to avoid any water getting into the dog's eyes.*

infection. Express the glands before you start washing the dog (see Chapter Six, page 45).

It is desirable to have a spray hose, such as the one shown in the photographs below, to facilitate the soaking and rinsing of the dog. Leaving the head until last, soak the dog all over with warm water, starting at the rear and working forward, paying particular attention to the anus. However, if the dog is infested with fleas, always wet and wash the head first. Once the dog has been completely soaked, take the shampoo and apply a little to the back, then each leg, the stomach and under the tail. Work up a good lather, massaging the skin. Once again, you should move from back to front and pay special attention to the anus and the pads. With a heavily-coated dog, take the small brush and, using a light, rearward motion, brush the shampoo into the fur. Rinse the dog from front to rear.

Repeat the shampooing process and continue rinsing until all traces of soap have been washed away. Next, hold up the dog's head and wash it using a 'tearless' or baby shampoo. Do not get soap into its eyes.

When rinsing is complete, a coat conditioner can be applied. A handful will be sufficient for a Labrador-sized dog. Work thoroughly through the fur, paying special attention to any areas which may be knotted. The conditioner must be rinsed out thoroughly.

Gently squeeze the hair on the legs, tail, ears and all parts of the dog's body to remove excess water. Then, using a sponge (kitchen sponges are excellent), rub the dog all over, then rub it briskly with the towel before finishing with the hair dryer.

1

2

3

Above: *Using a good quality shampoo of your choice, work the soap well in over the body to create a good, rich lather.*

Below: *Rinse the dog working from front to rear. Then repeat the shampooing process. Rinse until the water runs clear.*

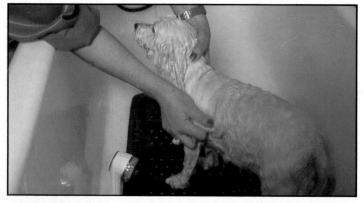

4

Below: *Wash the head using a baby or tearless shampoo. Take great care when washing around the eyes, but clean thoroughly.*

Right: *Rub the dog all over with a kitchen sponge. This will save you a lot of time and effort when you start the drying.*

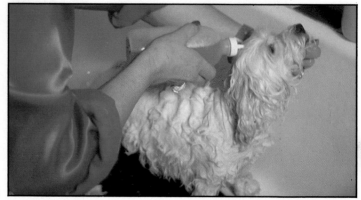

5

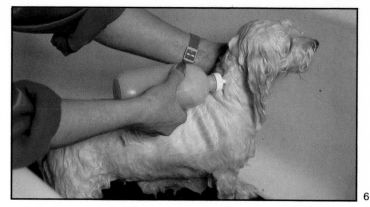

6

Above: *Apply a little conditioner to the hairiest parts, especially any matted areas. Leave it on for between one and two minutes.*

Below: *Give a final rinse to remove all traces of soap and conditioner. Gently squeeze out the excess water from the coat.*

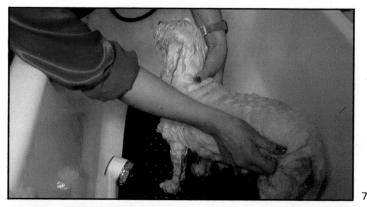

7

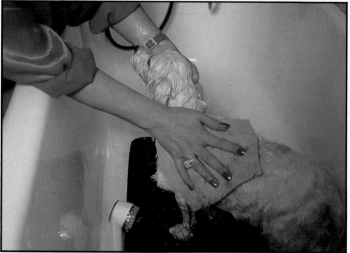

8

Chapter Five

DRYING

Equipment

Small hand-held hair dryer or Small/large professional canine power dryer or Large, professional cabinet dryer (able to dry two to six dogs), or towel bag; Collapsible or electric grooming table (optional); Grooming sling or restrainer (optional); Brush (pin or slicker)

Which method?

There are two different ways to dry your dog. Smooth-coated dogs and Terrier types can be placed in a dog 'towel bag' which zips up to the neck to absorb water from the coat, thus saving a lot of hard work. Finish drying the dog by hand – the alternative method of drying. For the latter method, a small, domestic, hand-held dryer will suffice, but a professional canine power dryer is quicker and easier to use and, in the long term, more economical.

Fluffy-coated dogs, especially Poodles and Bichon Frisés, need to be blow-dried by hand from start to finish, the purpose being to straighten the coat. However competent one becomes at the art of scissoring, a good finish will not be achieved unless the hair is blown completely straight before you begin any scissor work.

Hand drying

Stand your dog on a table, draining board or rubber mat (you can use the one from your bath). It is important to remember to direct the air flow onto the part of the body you are drying; otherwise you will waste time, energy and electricity. If you are using a domestic hair dryer, take care not to allow dog hair to clog the air intake.

With the brush in one hand and the dryer in the other, brush the hair upwards on the legs and forwards on the body. All hair should be brushed in the opposite direction to the way it falls. The aim is to straighten the hair as much as possible, so that it stands away from the body. For brushing fluffy-coated breeds, it is best to use a slicker brush. The brush should be held lightly – pressing too hard on the dog can cause a rash. If this does occur, dab on a little Witch Hazel. If the brush is dropped occasionally, this is a sign that it is being used correctly. Speed is another essential in hand drying to prevent the coat curling. If it shows signs of curling, damp the coat down with a little water.

When you think the dog is completely dry, re-check. In the heavily-coated breeds, the ears, featherings, and feet are frequently left damp, and when the dog is subsequently hand scissored, the final effect is spoiled. Allow the dog a relaxation period before the next stage – clipping, or scissoring (see Section Two).

Natural drying

Breeds such as the Puli, Komondor and the short-haired breeds may be left to dry naturally after being towel-dried, particularly on a warm day.

34

Above: *Three professional power dryers. These are far more powerful and easier to use than domestic, hand-held dryers.*

Below: *Place a good-sized towel around your dog. Place it on a table, draining board or rubber mat, depending on the dog's size.*

1

2

Above: *Using a towel, rub the coat gently but thoroughly to remove water, taking care to dry the featherings and feet.*

Below: *Ensure that the ears are towel-dried thoroughly – check that the cotton wool has been taken out of the ears.*

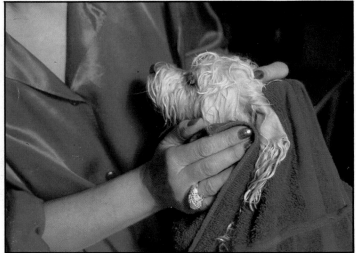

3

4

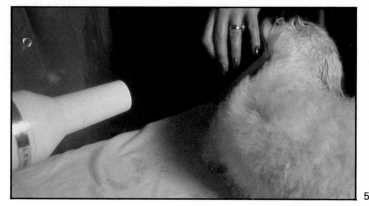

5

Above: *Remember to direct the flow of hot air onto the area you are brushing to dry it effectively and economically.*

Below: *You may need someone to hold the dryer while you brush if you are using a domestic dryer which is not free-standing.*

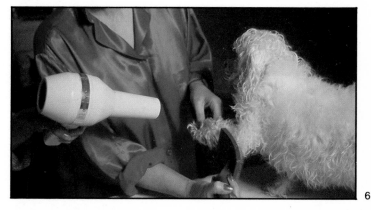

6

Below left: *Begin drying the coat. The hair should be brushed in the opposite direction to the way in which it falls.*

Below: *The aim of hand drying is to straighten the hair. It is important to work quickly to prevent the coat curling.*

7

8

Above: *Hold the brush lightly in your hand and flick the hair upwards and outwards to make it stand away from the body.*

Below: *Being gentle but firm, make your dog stand as you want it to, but never pull any limbs out from a natural position.*

9

Below: *When hand drying the face, use warm air while you brush - it will be uncomfortable for your dog if the air is too hot.*

Right: *This type of free-standing power dryer will enable you to use both hands - to hold the dog in position while you brush.*

10

11

Above: *Every part of the coat must be thoroughly dried. Damp down the coat with water if it shows signs of curling.*

Below: *Brush very gently under the stomach when drying, taking the utmost care not to scratch the nipples with the brush.*

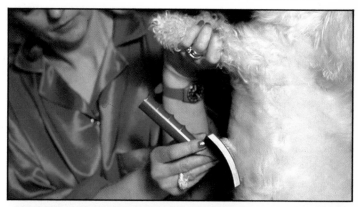

12

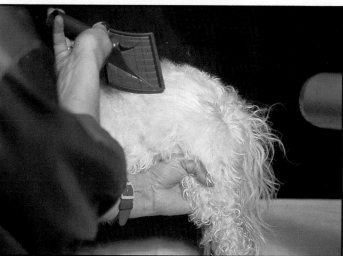

13

Chapter Six

WELFARE AND HEALTH CARE

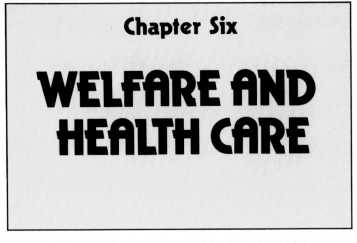

TEETH

— Equipment —
Soft toothbrush
Canine toothpaste

The puppy
Puppies are generally purchased at eight weeks old, and at this time they will still have their baby or 'milk' teeth, to be replaced by permanent teeth at six to seven months of age or older. Before the permanent teeth erupt, small amounts of fluoride can be given to beneficial effect – similar to a human baby's dose. Consult your veterinarian on your first visit. Check to see if the permanent teeth are pushing through the gums properly. Consult your veterinarian if problems develop.

It is advisable to introduce your puppy to teeth brushing at an early age, using a soft toothbrush and a canine toothpaste at least once a week. If your dog is highly intolerant of the brushing, try an application of hydrogen peroxide mouth wash or baking salt dissolved in water on a soft rag wrapped around your finger.

The adult
Dogs' teeth frequently accumulate tartar on the surface, particularly if they are fed only soft food. Hard-baked dog biscuits and marrow bones or chew bones all help with oral hygiene, but if tartar has accumulated, it must be scraped off. Many dogs do not take kindly to the treatment, so it is best to let your veterinarian regularly remove the tartar and polish the teeth under anesthetic.

Rather than attempting to use a dental scaler, you can purchase a finger stool with pumice powder to remove tartar from the teeth.

If your dog has smelly breath, loses teeth prematurely, if there are signs of decay or the gums are red and sore, then seek expert veterinary attention.

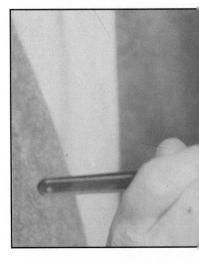

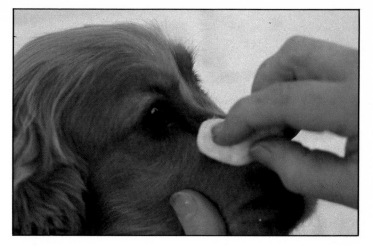

EYES

┌─────────────────────────┐
│ ──── **Equipment** ──── │
│ Cotton wool │
│ Eye lotion │
│ Cool water │
└─────────────────────────┘

Care procedure

A slight, clear discharge from the eyes is normal in many dogs, but in some breeds the shape of the eye will lead to a heavy discharge and staining of the hair surrounding the eye. This can be treated daily with a proprietory preparation, which will improve

Above: *If eyes are inflamed or discharging pus, bathe gently using a different piece of cotton wool for each eye to cleanse.*

the appearance of the eyes and reduce local skin problems.

Some breeds, such as the Pekingese, Shih Tzu, Japanese Chin and King Charles Spaniel have large, prominent eyes which can be scratched or irritated. If

Below: *If your pet will tolerate it, brush the teeth once a week using a soft toothbrush and a toothpaste specially for dogs.*

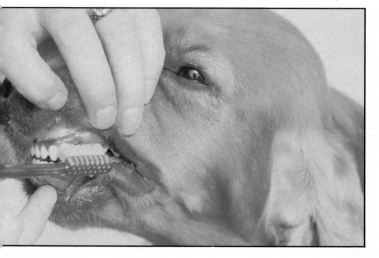

facial hairs curl into the eyes and irritate the cornea, they should carefully be plucked out with thumb and index finger.

If the eyes are inflamed or discharging pus, check for foreign bodies such as grass seeds, then bathe with cotton wool and cool water. If the discharge is heavy or persistent, veterinary advice should be sought immediately.

EARS

Equipment
Forceps
Cotton buds
or Cotton wool
Ear-cleaning fluid

Care procedure
Ears should be examined at least once a week to make sure they are pink, clean and sweet smelling. If there is any dark brown discharge or unpleasant odour, or if your dog persistently shakes its head or scratches its ears, seek veterinary help.

Keep the ears clean by using a piece of cotton wool or a cotton wool bud dipped in almond or olive oil, or a proprietory medicated ear-cleaning fluid.

Take care not to probe deep into the ear recess.

Many long-coated breeds, especially those with hanging ears, have hair growing inside their ears. This hair should be removed once every six weeks, before it grows too long and mats up, thereby restricting air circulation and causing infections, such as Canker. Dogs that shed their coats have little if any hair in the ears to be removed. To remove the hair, artery forceps are available from grooming suppliers to do the job, or the hair can be plucked out little by little using your thumb and finger. After removing the hair, gently clean the ear recess with a medicated ear-cleaning fluid.

Right: *The quick can be seen in this light-coloured nail. If the nail bleeds, apply a nail blood-clotting fluid.*

Below right: *Ears need to be checked and cleaned regularly with cotton wool and almond or olive oil, or medicated fluid.*

Below: *Holding the ear open with one hand, gently pluck a few hairs at a time. Do not probe into the ear recess.*

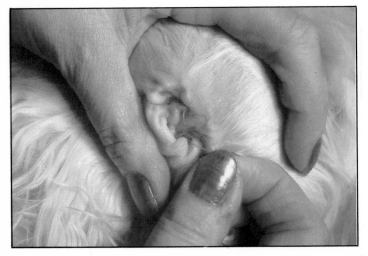

NAILS

Equipment

Nail clippers – guillotine
Nail file (optional)

When to trim
Dogs that enjoy regular road exercise rarely need their nails trimmed. Unfortunately, many house pets seldom get enough exercise. Consequently, their nails do not receive the natural grinding which comes with a reasonable amount of outdoor activity, and they have to be trimmed regularly using a pair of nail clippers. Use the guillotine type (see page 19).

The quick
Great care must be taken not to cut the soft, fleshy area inside the nail called the **quick**, which contains the nerves and blood supply; it will bleed profusely if cut. If a dog has ever been hurt in this way, it can make it wary of nail clipping for a very long time, and a second person may have to be enlisted to calm the dog, or the dog taken to a veterinarian for nail trimming. If you look closely at the nail, particularly if it is light or white in colour, the quick will show up clearly as a pink vein. If you do cause the nail to bleed, apply a nail blood-clotting solution. If your dog has dewclaws (an extra toe on the inside of the front legs), trim these in the same way.

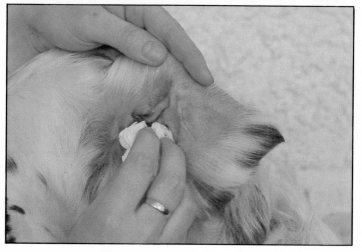

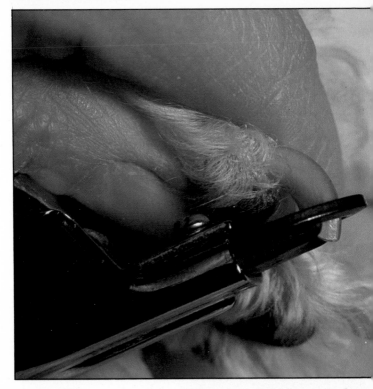

Above: *Hold the nail clippers in the correct position under the dog's foot. Stop cutting before you reach the quick.*

Below: *To empty glands, hold tail up and squeeze with finger and thumb either side of the anus, pushing towards the body.*

Nail trimming procedure

Sit the dog on a table facing you. Holding the paw firmly, trim the tips of the nails with short, decisive strokes. A small dog can be held firmly under the left arm, cutting the nails with the clippers in your right hand.

After the nails have been cut, you can use a nail file to smooth off any rough edges.

GLANDS

———— Equipment ————
Cotton wool

All dogs have two anal sacs which lie on either side of and just below the anus. These glands secrete a brownish-yellow, foul-smelling fluid. Occasionally, they become blocked, and unless expressed the fluid may become infected and an anal abscess can form.

Below: *Emptying the glands is best done in the bath before bathing, where the yellow-brown fluid can be washed away.*

Signs of impaction

If an owner sees his or her dog dragging its anus on the carpet or grass, this can be a sign of impacted glands. The dog may also turn round to inspect its back end frequently and suddenly, as a reaction to pain around the anus. Veterinary help should be sought.

Expressing the glands

In a situation where no abnormality is suspected, the owner can express the dog's anal glands approximately every eight weeks. This is best done when the dog is in the bath, before shampooing. Holding the dog's tail up with your left hand, squeeze either side of the anus with the finger and thumb of the right hand, pushing in towards the dog's body. Be gentle but firm. It is best to cover the anus with a pad of cotton wool before expressing the glands, as the accumulation usually spurts out. If you know a breeder, or you are on good terms with your veterinarian, ask for a demonstration. The normal secretion should be brownish-yellow in colour. If pus or blood appear, consult your veterinarian.

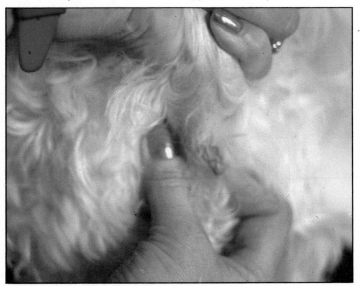

EXTERNAL PARASITES

Fleas

These are very common, and they are not particular about where they live or who they bite. They have increased with the advent of central heating and fitted carpets. Fleas do not need to live on you or your pet; they just need a warm-blooded body to feed off when they are hungry. Because they are small and active, you may not actually see them. But you can spot where they have been by noticing the dark brown droppings when you are grooming, particularly around the neck and on the stomach.

Flea control is an important part of grooming. Fleas can cause skin problems if your pet is allergic to their bite, and they can also cause you to have irritating red spots. Insecticidal shampoos and flea sprays are easy to apply and effective. Insecticides are also now available which actually inhibit flea reproduction – a great advance. It is vital to treat your dog and its environment at the same time. When using insecticides, follow the manufacturer's instructions carefully. These products must kill the fleas but not the host.

Ticks

Dogs can pick up ticks by running through grass, woods or sandy beaches. These blood-sucking insects bury their barbed mouths firmly into the dog's skin, causing irritation and often resulting in secondary skin infections. To remove adult ticks, soak them with ether, surgical

Below: *These are the common external dog parasites with their eggs. The follicular mite, which is invisible to the naked eye, causes demodectic mange. This condition shows as bald patches sometimes with pustules. Seek veterinary advice without delay.*

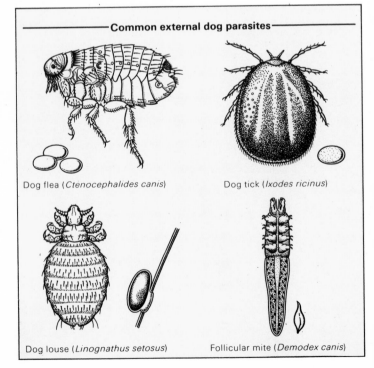

Common external dog parasites

Dog flea (*Ctenocephalides canis*)

Dog tick (*Ixodes ricinus*)

Dog louse (*Linognathus setosus*)

Follicular mite (*Demodex canis*)

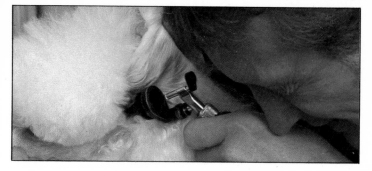

Above: *A vet examines the deep ear with an auriscope. Mites can live here on skin debris.*

spirit or tick spray. This will loosen the head and mouthparts to enable the removal of the whole insect with tweezers. The dog can be regularly bathed in a 'tick dip' to prevent infestation, especially if it is in contact with sheep. The dog's environment should be vigorously disinfected as in some countries ticks transmit serious diseases and can cause tick paralysis.

Lice (pediculosis)

Lice are spread by direct contact or by contaminated brushes and combs. They accumulate under mats of hair around the ears, neck and body openings causing intense irritation. Since the insects are only $\frac{1}{10}$in (3mm) long, they are difficult to see. If you suspect infestation, bathe your dog using an insecticidal shampoo at weekly intervals and clip matted hair away. Lice live and breed entirely on the dog, so it is not important to treat the dog's environment, such as his bed, as well.

Ear mites

These parasites live on skin debris on the surface of the ear canal. They can cause intense irritation and the production of reddish brown crusts. The infection is highly contagious and is especially prevalent in young animals. Mineral oils combined with an insecticide are effective as long as the treatment is maintained for a four-week period. The dog's environment should be treated as thoroughly as the dog itself.

Cheyletiella mites (walking dandruff)

This is a parasite that can cause unpleasant irritation to the owner as well as the pet host. The mites live only on the host and consequently are easier to deal with. The mites and eggs can be seen with a magnifying lens, but the appearance of fine dandruff on the coat gives a clue to their presence. Most insecticides are effective but should be applied three times at weekly intervals.

Scabies (sarcoptic mange)

This mite produces an intensely itchy, non-seasonal, transmissible infection. The mites burrow in the superficial layers of the skin, and can live on human beings for at least six days. The infection is highly contagious and young animals are particularly susceptible.

As the mite lives most of its life below the surface of the skin, it can be difficult to diagnose, even by repeated skin scrapings examined microscopically. Your veterinarian may make a diagnosis purely on the appearance of the patient. Although insecticides are effective, hair will need to be clipped away and other medications used to relieve irritation and remove skin scale. Again, the dog's environment should be treated with an insecticide at the same time.

Chapter Seven

FINISHING TOUCHES

RIBBONS AND BOWS

Making your own ribbons and bows is very easy and can be great fun. They add a special finishing touch to your smartly groomed canine companion. When you begin making them, you are sure to invent many different designs of your own.

Below: *Making your own ribbons can be great fun. You can invent many different shapes and styles according to your preference, like these attractive examples.*

Florists' ribbon is probably the best type to use and the most economical.

Where to tie
Bows look best tied to the ear feathering, where the ear meets the topknot, eg in the Poodle (see pages 15 and 75). Attach a bow to one or both ears. Ribbons can also be used in the middle of the topknot (with the Poodle, this would flatten the topknot), eg in the Yorkshire Terrier to tie back the profuse facial hair (see page 54).

Follow this photographic sequence to make a basic bow.

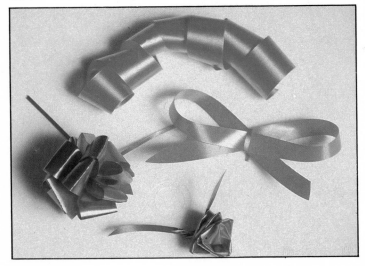

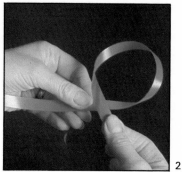

Above: *To make a plain bow, cut a straight piece of ribbon about 6in (15cm) and ½in (12mm) wide, depending on the dog's size.*

Above: *Cross one end of the piece of ribbon over the other to form a fairly large loop, and then hold it in place.*

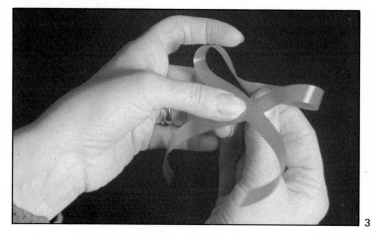

Above: *Grasp the top of the loop in the middle and bend back down to meet the point where the two ends of the ribbon cross.*

Below: *Secure the middle of the bow with a dab of glue, or tie in place with a thin strip of ribbon – see bow on page 48.*

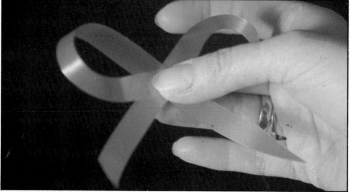

Section Two

STEP-BY-STEP GROOMING

Smooth coats:
Great Dane; Chihuahua 52

Straight, silky coats:
Toy Terriers – Maltese; Yorkshire Terrier 53
Afghan Hound 55

Woolly, curly coats:
Poodle – Teddy Bear Trim 58
Poodle – Lamb Clip 64
Bichon Frisé 76

Harsh with undercoat:
Old English Sheepdog 84

Handstrip coats:
Border Terrier – Handstripped 92
Spaniels – Handstripped 98
West Highland White Terrier – Clipped 102
Spaniels – Clipped 110

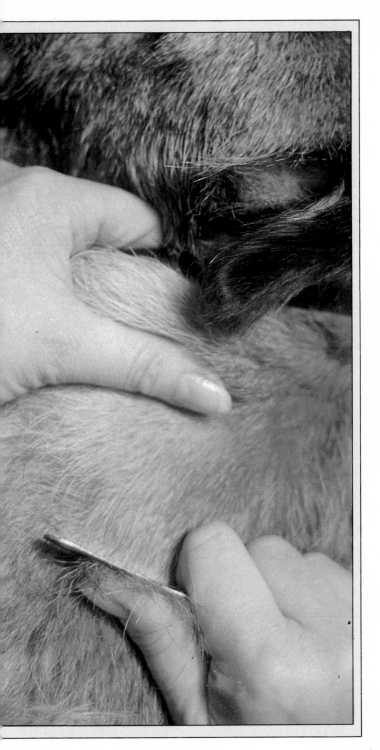

Coat type: Smooth

GREAT DANE CHIHUAHUA

Equipment:
Hound glove
Bristle brush
Coat dressing (optional)
Chamois leather (optional)

The smooth-coated breeds are the easiest to groom. It is just a question of the amount of coat area you have to cover – from the tiny Chihuahua to the aptly-named Great Dane. They require only a thorough brushing with a rubber hound glove or bristle brush once or twice a week, depending on your available time.

An occasional bath is all that is required – plus an application of a coat dressing once or twice a week, which imparts a pleasant smell and a lovely sheen to the dog's coat. The coat can also be rubbed briskly with a chamois cloth for extra gloss.

Below: *The Great Dane and the Chihuahua may be at opposite ends of the size scale, but their grooming needs are the same.*

Coat type: Straight, silky (Toys)

TOY TERRIERS

Maltese, Yorkshire Terrier

Equipment:
Bristle brush   Comb
Coat dressing (optional)
For scissored style only:
Scissors   Clippers
Clipper blade No 7f (or equivalent)
Thinning scissors   Ribbon (optional)

Long, natural style

These Toy breeds, when kept in full coat, need daily brushing and combing since this type of coat is inclined to tangle. A soft, bristle brush is recommended for daily use, but if you have problems with a tangled coat, you may need to revert to a slicker brush. To free the mats, damp down the coat with a de-matting solution and gently tease them out.

The body coat of the Maltese and Yorkie is parted down the middle of the back from the base of the skull to the base of the tail. Comb the hair and spray with coat dressing, which will help to set the parting and enhance the healthy shine of the coat.

The topknot of both breeds is best tied up with a ribbon.

Short style

This style is practical, being much easier to maintain, yet smart and appealing. The body coat is clipped with a No 7f blade, while the legs and head – including the brows – are scissored, and thinning scissors used to blend with the clipped areas.

Below: *Varying styles for silky-coated Toy breeds. Left and right (Yorkie) clipped and scissored; the Maltese is left long.*

Above: *This style is practical and appealing. The body has been clipped with a No 7f blade, the legs and head scissored and the hair blended with the clipped areas using thinning scissors.*

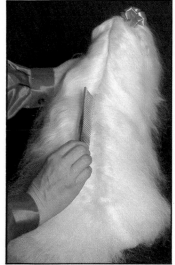

Right: *This Maltese has been bathed, conditioned and blow dried. The long hair is then parted from the head all the way down the back. The hair must be thoroughly combed; the coat can then be sprayed with a dressing.*

Below: *If you want to keep the head hair long and natural, draw a section of the hair up away from the eyes and secure with a ribbon. Alternatively, the brow hair can be scissored as in the photograph on page 53.*

Coat type: Straight, silky

AFGHAN HOUND

Equipment:
Pin brush
Coat dressing
Medium-toothed comb
Clippers
Clipper blade Nos 10, 15

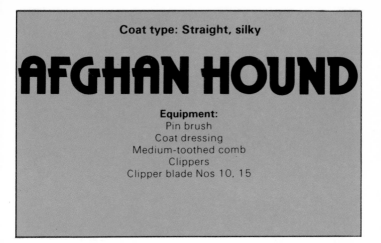

This is a breed which must be groomed every day. The soft, dense, silky coat is especially prone to matting, and it takes a dedicated owner to ensure the coat is kept in top condition.

Bathing an Afghan Hound is heavy work – the coat must be rinsed thoroughly and the profuse hair makes this a lengthy business. But if the dog is brushed strictly every day, to keep dirt and tangles at bay, bathing need only be undertaken four to six times a year. A pin brush is recommended for general use, but use a slicker brush for a neglected coat.

Grooming procedure
Feet Use your clippers with a No 10 or No 15 blade to remove any long hair from between the pads.

Groin Use a No 10 blade to clip the hair away from this area.

Body and legs Start brushing from the stomach area using a downward and outward motion. Continue brushing thoroughly up the side of the legs. When the entire coat has been brushed, gently comb through the hair.

Head Part the hair on the head down the middle and comb through.

Below: *Begin by removing any excess hair from between the pads using the clippers with a No 10 or a No 15 clipper blade.*

1

2

Above: *Use a No 10 blade to clip hair away from the groin, taking care to avoid pressure around the nipples in a female.*

Below: *Starting from the stomach area, lift the top hair with one hand and brush the remaining hair with a down and out motion.*

3

Below: *Work up the side of the legs, brushing out thoroughly. Hold the leg out at an angle to brush beneath the elbow.*

Right: *Grooming over, the silky coat of the Afghan – surely the most beautiful in the canine world – gleams to perfection.*

4

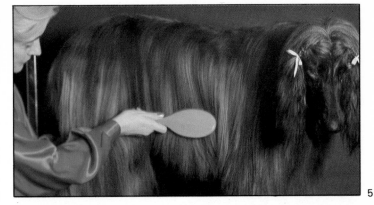

5

Above: *You should be able to brush through the coat with no resistance. Use a slicker brush on a neglected coat.*

Below: *Use a metal comb for the head. Here, the hair should be parted and left to hang naturally, framing the face.*

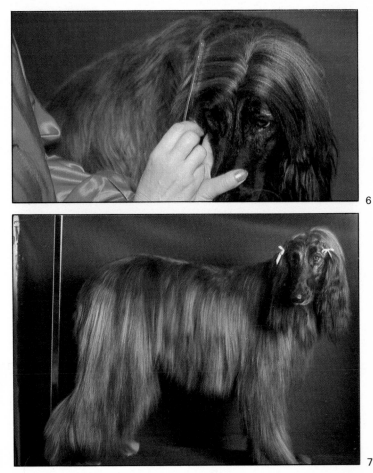

6

7

Coat type: Woolly, curly

POODLE

Style 2: Teddy Bear Trim

Equipment:
Slicker brush
Comb
Scissors

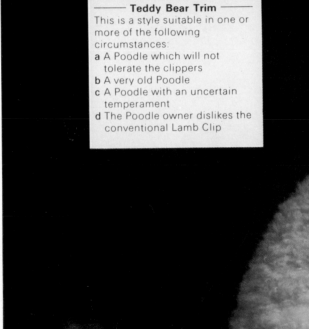

———— **Teddy Bear Trim** ————
This is a style suitable in one or
more of the following
circumstances:
a A Poodle which will not
  tolerate the clippers
b A very old Poodle
c A Poodle with an uncertain
  temperament
d The Poodle owner dislikes the
  conventional Lamb Clip

Grooming procedure
Begin by thoroughly combing the dog.

Body and legs Starting with the back legs, scissor off all wispy ends to give a smooth, rounded finish, scissoring a little at a time. Scissor all over the body, down the inside and outside of the front legs, blending the hair to a plush finish. While holding the tail up with one hand, scissor the hair around the hindquarters to a fairly short length.

Tail Scissor the tail to whatever shape you prefer to make it neat and smart – you do not have to have a pompon with this style.

Feet Scissor neatly around each paw – shape the feet round.

Head Lifting up the ears, scissor to a neat length the hair in the underlying area. Scissor the hair across the eyes. Trim a little hair from the bottom of the ears at the front. Carefully trim away any long hair from the inside corners of the eyes, if necessary. Round off the head with the scissors to the particular shape that appeals to you and which in your opinion suits your dog.

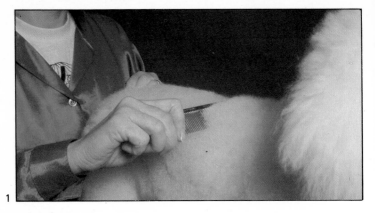

1

Above: *Begin by thoroughly combing the dog. Instructions for the Bichon Frisé are applicable here, apart from clipper work.*

Right: *Holding the tail, scissor the hair fairly short around the hindquarters. This will help to keep an older dog clean.*

2

Above: *Starting with the back legs, scissor a little hair at a time, making sure you cut off all wispy ends.*

Below: *Scissor the body of the dog to an even length all over to give a well-groomed, smooth and natural look.*

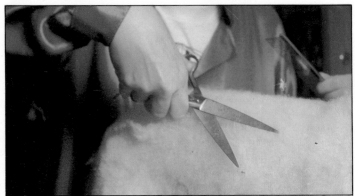

3

Above: *Scissor up the inside of the front legs, remembering to keep the blades of the scissors flat against the hair.*

Below: *Perfecting your scissoring will take time. A contrasting background will help you to get a neat outline.*

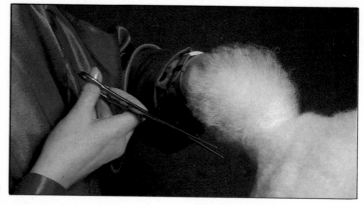

Above: *The pompon tail is optional with this clip. This tail is scissored to an even length all over, to blend with the body.*

Below: *Trim a little hair from the bottom front side of the ear, and from the corner of the eyes, if this is necessary.*

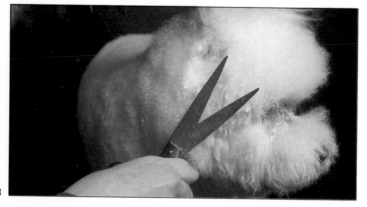

Below: *Scissor the hair straight across above the eyes. Be very careful when scissoring in this area, for obvious reasons.*

Right: *The finished Teddy Bear Trim has been set off with a pink bow to provide a counterpoint to this Poodle's white coat.*

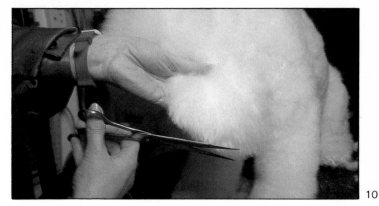

Above: *Lift the ears and scissor the edges and underneath to make each ear lie close to the head in a natural position.*

Below: *Finally, scissor over the head, rounding it to the desired shape and taking care to cut off all wispy hair.*

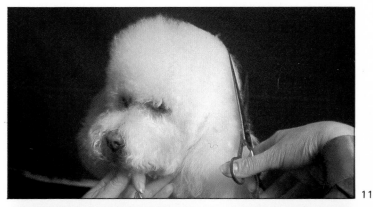

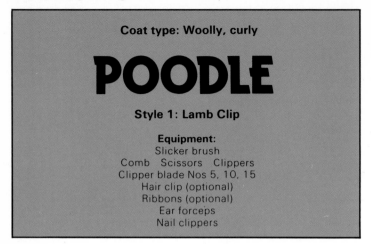

Coat type: Woolly, curly

POODLE

Style 1: Lamb Clip

Equipment:
Slicker brush
Comb   Scissors   Clippers
Clipper blade Nos 5, 10, 15
Hair clip (optional)
Ribbons (optional)
Ear forceps
Nail clippers

The Lamb Clip is one of the most popular for the pet Poodle. It is practical, smart and very easy to manage.

It is best to clip the face, feet, tail base and groin prior to bathing (see Grooming Procedure below). The nails should also be trimmed. Empty the anal glands, if necessary, during the bathing process (see Chapter Six). The coat must then be thoroughly dried following the detailed instructions for hand drying in Chapter Five, and the entire coat combed before continuing with the clipping and scissoring.

The Poodle is a breed which grows hair inside the ears. Pluck this hair out after bathing (see Chapter Six).

Grooming procedure
Before bathing
Face See diagram of the Poodle's head. Clip the face **against** the lie of the coat using a No 10 clipper blade from the ear to the outer corner of the eye, on both sides of the head. Clip off the hair from the throat and chin starting from the corner of the ear down to the Adam's Apple in a 'V' or 'U' shape. Holding the jaws together, clip each side of the muzzle gently and slowly, pulling back the corners of the mouth to avoid nicking the loose skin with the clippers. Use parallel strokes to clip down the inner corner of the eyes, along the top of the muzzle to the nose.

Feet Use a No 10 or No 15 blade to clip the feet **against** the lie of the hair. Finish at the end of the foot, ie ½–1in (1–2.5cm) above the pads. To clip between the toes, place one finger between the pads underneath the foot and simultaneously spread open the toes with your thumb. Holding clippers flat, use the edge of the blade to clip between the toes in a scooping motion, first on one side and then the other. Do not point the entire blade into the webbing; you may nick the skin. You should also remove the hair between the pads on the bottom.

Groin Clip away the hair from this area using a No 10 blade.

Tail base The tail should be roughly three-quarters pompon and a quarter clipped. Clipping against the growth of the hair, using a No 10 blade, clip about 1½in (3.5cm) of tail depending on its length.

After bathing
Body and legs Start clipping **with** the lie of the coat from the base of the skull down and around the neck using a No 5 blade. Continue along the back to the base of the tail. Clip down

over the ribs following the contours of the body (see diagram for clipping pattern). Lift the front right leg and clip beneath the chest and under the stomach on that side. Repeat with left leg; clip on left side.

Begin with either hindleg and comb the hair downwards towards the feet. Scissor off any wispy hair to make a neat line all round the foot. Complete all feet in this way. Return to the front legs and comb the hair outwards. Extending one leg at a time, scissor off all loose ends from the inside of the leg to achieve a smooth, uniform surface. Then scissor off stray ends in the same way from the outside of the legs. Trimming a little at a time, blend the longer hair at the top of the front legs towards the shoulders into the short, clipped body hair.

Below: *For the Lamb Clip, the body, face and feet are clipped. Follow the direction of the arrows with your clippers.*

With the hindquarters facing you, shape the hindleg evenly all over with the scissors following the angulation of the leg. Gradually work upwards and blend the hair at the top of the hindquarters with the clipped body hair. Hold the tail to one side and scissor under the tail.

Tail Comb the hair towards the top of the tail. Slide your fingers to the end of the tail bone and scissor straight across the ends of the hair. Holding the end of the tail, shape into a pompon scissoring a little at a time.

Head Turn the dog towards you and, while holding the muzzle, comb the hair to one side and scissor over the top of the ear. Then scissor the front of the 'topknot' evenly across the eyes. Blend the clipped hair at the base of the skull into the topknot. Round off the topknot to a smooth shape, leaving more hair in the centre of the head, tapering to the sides.

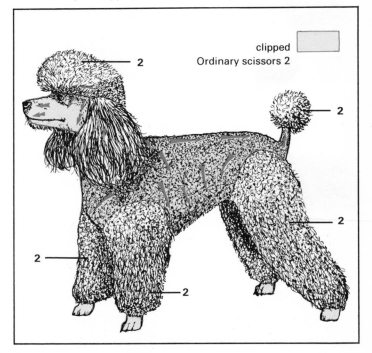

clipped

Ordinary scissors 2

2
2
2
2
2

Above: *This dog is ready for clipping. Usually the face, feet, tail and groin areas are clipped before the dog is bathed.*

Below: *Using a No 10 blade, clip the face against the lie of the coat, working from the corner of the ear to the eye.*

1

2

Above: *Clip from the Adam's Apple up, removing hair from the throat and chin. Leave a rounded 'U' or 'V'-shaped line around the front of the neck, and scissor off any wispy hair.*

Below and bottom: *Pull back the mouth to avoid nicking the sensitive skin, and clip the muzzle. Clip down from the corner of the eye to the nose with parallel strokes.*

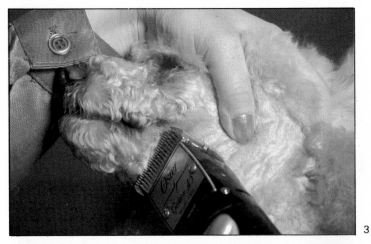

3

4

5

Above: *Use a 10 or 15 blade on the feet and, as on the face, clip against the lie of the hair. Never dig the blade into the skin.*

Right: *Clip the hair from the groin and stomach area, using a No 10 clipper blade. Stop when you reach the ribcage.*

6

Above: *Spread the toes apart with one finger under the webbing. Use the blade edge to clip hair between the toes.*

Below: *Clip only to the end of the foot, approximately ½–1in (12–25mm) above the pads. You should avoid clipping the ankle.*

7

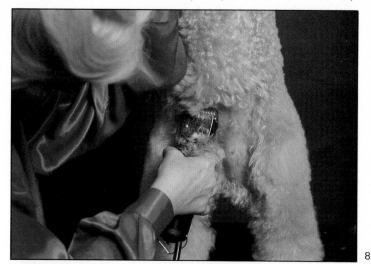

8

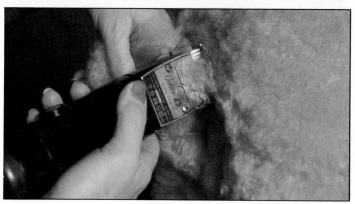

9

Above: *This clip needs a good pompon tail. Use a No 10 blade against the growth, and clip away about 1½in (37mm).*

Below: *Using a No 5 blade, clip the hair from the base of the skull down and around the neck, along the lie of the coat.*

10

11

Above: *Continue to clip down the back of the dog to the base of the tail, making sure the hair is an even length all over.*

Above right: *When clipping the hind leg, place the hindquarters facing you, and begin by combing down towards the foot.*

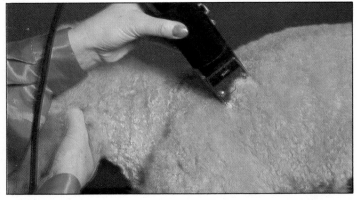

12

Above: *Look at the pattern in the diagram on page 65, and clip down over the ribs, following the contours of the body.*

Below: *Lift the front leg to clip beneath the chest and under the stomach. Repeat with the other side.*

13

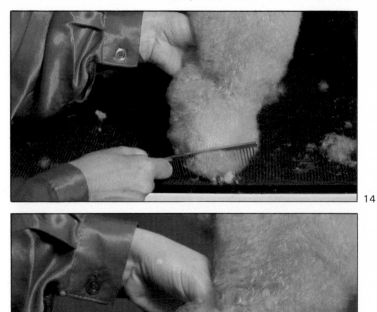

14

15

Above: *Scissor off any wispy hair to leave an even line all round the ankle at the point where it joins the foot.*

Below: *Comb the hair on the front leg outwards. Hold the leg and scissor off all uneven ends until you have a uniform surface.*

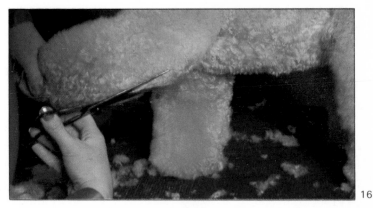

16

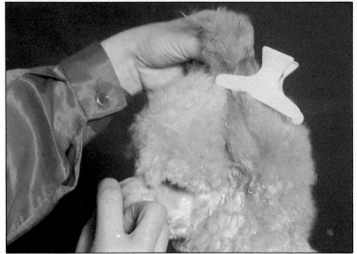

18

19

Above: *Blend the longer hair on the shoulders into the short, clipped body area, trimming a little of the hair at a time.*

Below: *Shape the hindlegs evenly all over. Be guided by the dog's conformation and scissor to show the angle above the hocks.*

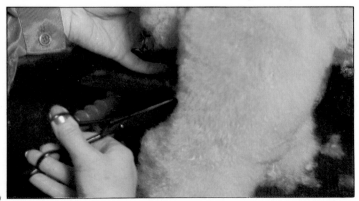

20

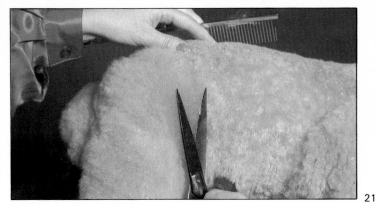

21

Left: *When scissoring the shoulders, it is helpful to use a hair clip as illustrated here, to hold the ears out of the way.*

Above: *As you gradually work upwards, use your scissors to blend the hair at the top of the hindquarters with the body hair.*

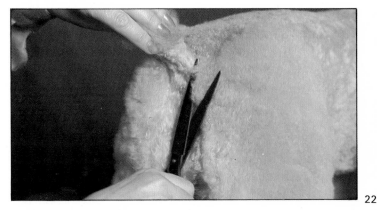

22

Above: *Scissor the area around the tail. Hold it to one side to enable you to scissor away the hair from underneath the tail.*

Below: *Comb the hair towards the tail tip. Slide fingers to the end of the tail bone and scissor hair straight across the ends.*

23

Above: *Holding the end of the tail and trimming the hair a little at a time, scissor the tail into a round, pompon shape.*

Below: *Turn the dog towards you and, holding the muzzle, comb the topknot hair to one side and scissor over the top of the ear.*

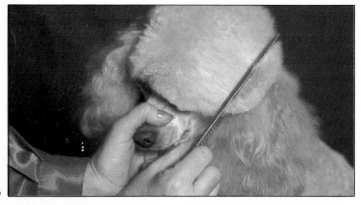

Below: *Scissor the front of the topknot evenly, just above the eyes; removing too much hair will spoil the dog's expression.*

Right: *The finished Poodle. Ribbons tied at the point where the ears meet the topknot will enhance the dog's appearance.*

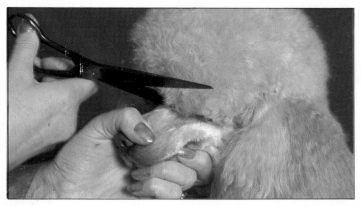

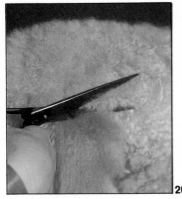

Above: *Using your scissors, blend the clipped hair at the base of the skull into the longer hair of the topknot as shown.*

Above: *The topknot should look rounded, but the hair in the centre slightly longer and fuller, tapering at the sides.*

Coat type: Woolly, curly

BICHON FRISÉ

Equipment:
Slicker brush
Comb
Scissors
Clippers (optional)
Clipper blade No 10 (optional)

Optional clipper work

Face If the eye staining is severe, clip away the hair from the inside corner of the eyes using a No 10 blade.

Pads Clip away any excess hair from between the pads.

Groin An optional, hygienic measure is to clip the groin area using the No 10 blade.

Scissoring

Body and legs Comb the coat thoroughly. In scissoring the pet Bichon, the length of coat is a matter of personal preference. The important point is to achieve an all-over roundedness. Scissor a little hair away from around the feet to give a neat line. Scissor away all wispy ends from the legs to give a neat, straight line up the inside of the legs. Following the angulation of the hindlegs, scissor rounding off all the time. The legs should all appear tubular (see diagram).

Scissor about ½in (12mm) around the root of the tail to set it off, and round off the hindquarters. Scissor along the back attempting to make the line of the back (the topline) straight. Scissor up to the shoulders, down over the ribs, underneath the stomach, round the neck, under the ears and down to the throat.

Right: The Bichon's topknot (hair on the head) is scissored to achieve a domed shape. Legs are rounded to look tubular.

Head Holding the ears up, scissor away a little hair from the area that lies beneath the ears. Cut away just a little of the hair under the chin.

The Bichon's topknot has a domed look. The hair increases in length towards the centre and back of the skull, and tapers to the sides. Cut the hair above the eyes and round off the head to achieve a smooth, domed shape. Scissor down straight over the top of the ears; do not cut the hair across the top of the ears where they join the head, as in the Poodle. The sides of the face are scissored to enhance the rounded look, and blended into the topknot hair. You should also scissor slightly across the bridge of the nose. Comb out the ear fringes, trimming them level with the chin hair.

Tail The Bichon's tail is one of its prize features; it should never be scissored.

Right: Scissor the coat of your pet Bichon to whatever length you find manageable. Try to achieve an all-over roundedness.

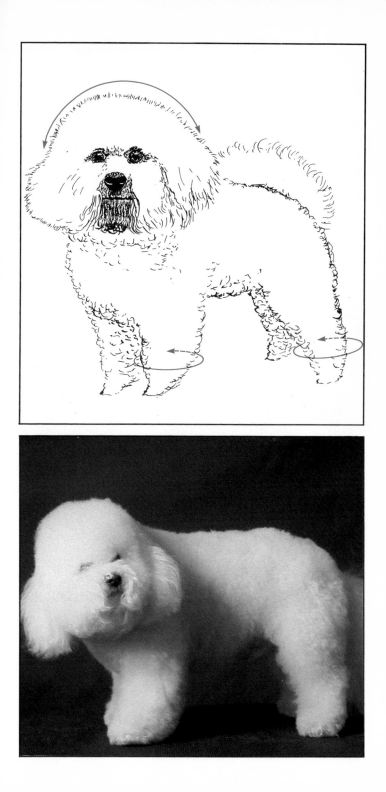

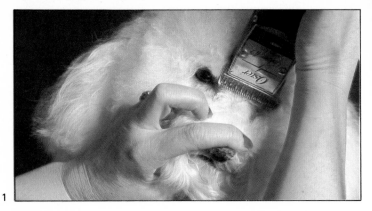

1

Above: *If staining is severe, clip away the hair from the inner corners of the eyes. Use a No 10 clipper blade for this purpose.*

Right: *Before you embark on any of the scissor work, you must spend some time thoroughly combing through the coat.*

2

Above: *Using the edge of the clipper blade (a No 10), carefully clip away any unwanted hair from between each of the pads.*

Below: *An optional hygienic measure, particularly with male dogs, is to clip the groin area using a No 10 clipper blade.*

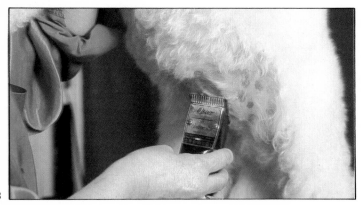

3

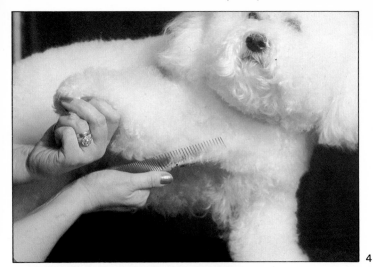

4

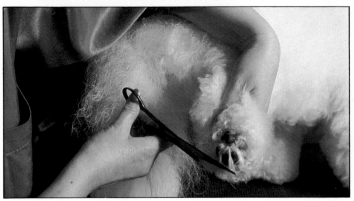

5

Above: *Scissor only a little hair from around the feet, just to give a neat base for working on the scissoring of the legs.*

Below: *Scissor away all the wispy ends until you have achieved a neat, straight line up the insides of both the hindlegs.*

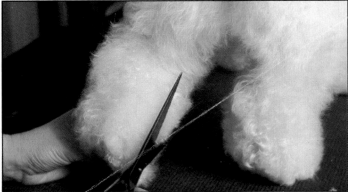

6

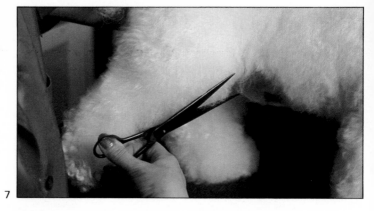

7

Above: *Follow the angulation of the hindlegs, rounding off all the time to give a tubular effect. Scissoring takes time to perfect.*

Below: *Scissor about ½ inch (12mm) around the root of the tail, to set it off. Round off the hindquarters with the scissors.*

8

Below: *Try and get a straight topline. Scissor to shoulder; the further back you stop, the longer the neck will appear.*

Right: *Holding the ears up with one hand, use your other hand to scissor away a little of the hair which lies beneath the ears.*

9

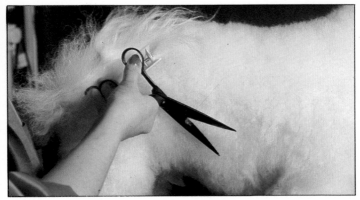

10

Above: *Carry on scissoring down and over the ribs and also right underneath the stomach, taking care not to nick the nipples.*

Below: *Scissor right round the neck, going under the ears and continuing down to the throat, rounding off all the time.*

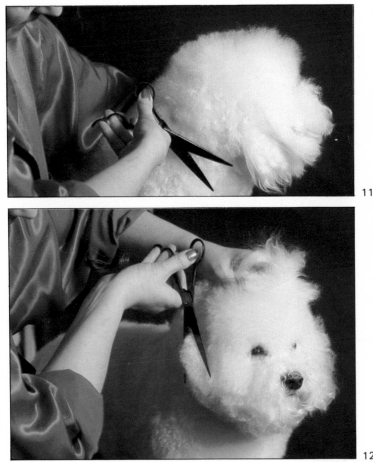

11

12

Above: *While still holding the ears up well out of the way, use your scissors to take off just a little hair under the chin.*

Below: *Always scissor straight down over the top of the ears with the Bichon; never across the top as you do with the Poodle.*

Below: *While holding the dog's head steady under its chin, scissor away the hair from above the eyes in a straight line.*

Right: *The well-groomed Bichon is a delight. Remember never to trim the Bichon's tail - it is one of the breed's best features.*

16

Above: *Round off the head to a domed shape, scissoring away all the wispy ends a little at a time to achieve a crisp outline.*

Below: *Thoroughly comb through the ear fringes. Scissor the ends only a little, to make them level with the hair on the chin.*

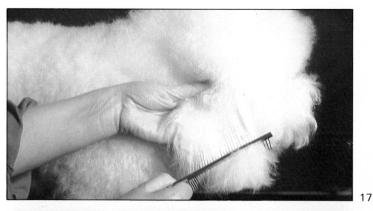

17

18

Coat type: Harsh with undercoat

OLD ENGLISH SHEEPDOG

Equipment:
Medium-toothed comb   Pin brush
Hair slide (optional)
For scissored style only:
Slicker brush   Scissors
Thinning scissors   Clippers
Clipper blade Nos 10 or 15

Full, natural style

If left in full coat, the old English Sheepdog must be brushed every day using a pin brush. Bear in mind that the 'Bobtail' will not get its adult coat fully until it is between two and three years of age. Brushing is a lengthy job with this breed, but its coat will mat very easily if this is not carried out daily. Comb through after brushing, separating the strands of the coat. A hair slide can be used to keep the loose hair on the head from falling into the eyes and possibly causing irritation.

Scissored style

The second style shown here is where the dog has been bathed, brushed and its coat scissored to a manageable length. The dog should be blow/hand dried (see Chapter Five) – a slicker brush used here may give a better finish when the coat is scissored. Brush the coat thoroughly paying special attention to the underarms, inside the legs and ears. Comb through the entire coat to make sure it is totally knot-free using a medium-toothed comb.

Face It is optional to trim the hair from the inner corners of the eyes with thinning scissors or ordinary scissors to prevent irritation.

Pads Use either a No 10 or 15 blade to remove hair from between and under the pads.

Groin Clip hair from the groin area by lifting up the hindleg.

Legs Start with the front legs, combing downwards and scissor all round, trimming around the edge of the foot to give a rounded look. Scissor the hindlegs following the natural angulation.

Body Scissor the shoulders, back and sides of the body to blend with the scissored legs. Following the body's contours, scissor underneath the stomach.

Head Hold up the ears and scissor the underlying hair downwards. Scissor under the chin and around the head, using thinning scissors to remove the hair across the eyes.

Right: *The scissored style is suitable for those owners of Old English Sheepdogs who do not want their pets clipped but wish to reduce the intensive, daily grooming necessary with a full-coated dog. This Old English Sheepdog has been bathed and blow dried, and is now ready for thorough brushing and combing prior to being scissored.*

1

Above: *Brush out the coat thoroughly. Pay special attention to neglected areas, ie under the arms, inside the legs and ears.*

Right: *Clip the hair from the inner corner of each eye. This is optional but can help reduce eye staining and prevent irritation.*

2

Above: *To achieve a good, even finish on a hand-scissored dog, the coat should be brushed until it is totally free of knots or mats.*

Below: *After brushing, comb the entire coat with a medium-toothed comb, drawing the hair up and away from the skin.*

3

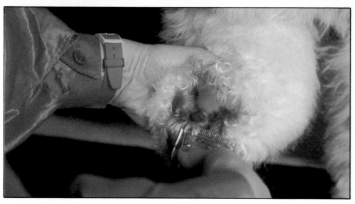

Above: *Using a No 10 or 15 blade, remove hair from between and under pads. Mats between toes can cause skin abrasions.*

Below: *Lift up the hindleg to facilitate the clipping of the hair from the groin area. Use a No 10 blade for this purpose.*

7

Above: *A final comb through before the scissor work. Do not be discouraged if early attempts at scissoring are uneven.*

Below: *Comb hair downwards and trim around the edge of the front feet removing any stray hairs. Aim for a rounded look.*

8

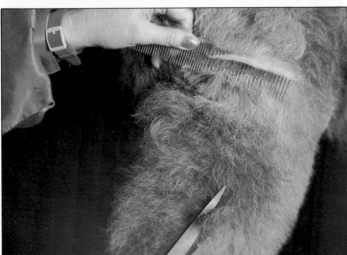

9

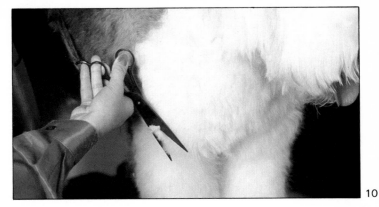

10

Above: *Scissor the shoulders, the hair on the back and sides to blend with the legs. Scissor to the same length of hair all over.*

Below: *While bearing in mind the shape of the body, use your scissors to cut and neaten the hair underneath the stomach.*

11

Left: *When scissoring the hair on the hindlegs, comb downwards and scissor a little at a time following the natural angulation.*

Below: *When the art of scissoring has been mastered, your dog's coat can be scissored to the desired length and shape.*

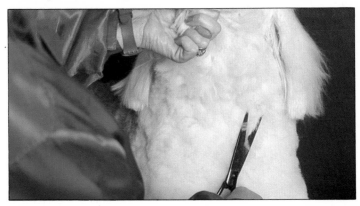

12

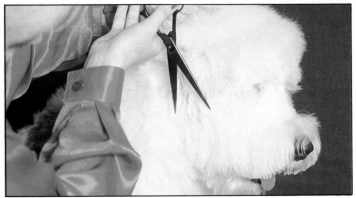

13

Above: *Lift up the ear flaps with one hand and cut away a little of the underlying hair with your scissors, pointing them down.*

Right: *The completed Old English Sheepdog, scissored to a manageable length. The end result is neat and stylish.*

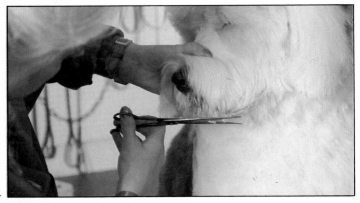

14

Above: *While holding the dog's head steady, scissor the hair over the entire head. Hold the muzzle to scissor under the chin.*

Below: *Use the thinning scissors to achieve a softer finish on the head – preferable when scissoring hair across the eyes.*

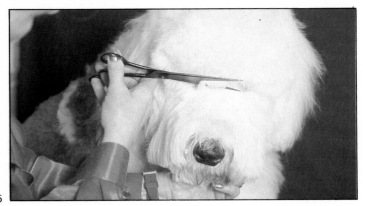

15

16

Below: *This Old English Sheepdog has been left unclipped; just bathed, blow dried and brushed.*

Below: *With the full-coated Old English Sheepdog, you can use a hair slide – one for humans! – to secure the hair above the eyes.*

17

18

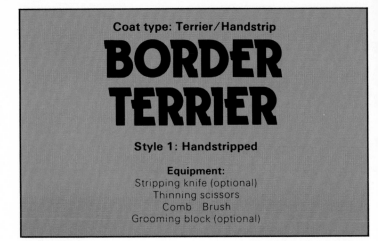

Coat type: Terrier/Handstrip

BORDER TERRIER

Style 1: Handstripped

Equipment:
Stripping knife (optional)
Thinning scissors
Comb Brush
Grooming block (optional)

Handstripping

Handstripping involves pulling out dead hair to give the coat a natural look typical of the breed. Because this technique is very time-consuming many owners of breeds that require stripping, ie Terriers and Spaniels, prefer to clip them every two months. If, however, you are prepared to put in the work, the results are most rewarding – the coat retains its true colour and texture. There are two methods of stripping:

1 The hair is gently plucked out between the finger and thumb in the direction of its growth.
2 The hair is plucked out with the

Below: Area to be handstripped. If using a knife, use quick, firm jerks and pull in the direction of hair growth.

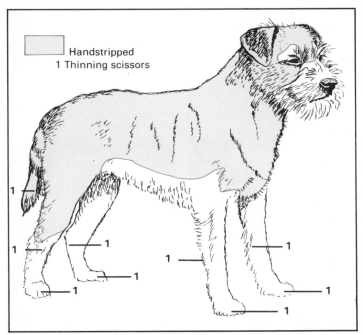

Handstripped
1 Thinning scissors

1
1 1
1 1
1
1 1
1
1

aid of a stripping knife. Use your free hand to carefully stretch the skin taut in front of the area you are working on. At the same time, push a small section of hair upwards and grasp between the knife and thumb.

If handstripping is carried out correctly, it will not cause the dog any discomfort. I would recommend you study your dog's Breed Standard before you begin work if you wish to retain the breed's characteristics. Always strip your dog **before** bathing.

Grooming procedure
Body and legs The entire coat of the Border Terrier is handstripped (excluding the moustache and eyebrows). Gently pluck away any stray ends on the underside of the tail with your finger and thumb. Scissor any wispy hairs from the feet or backs of the legs.

Head Gently strip out the hair from the top of the head, cheeks and ears, leaving the eyebrows and moustache.

Below: *This Border Terrier is ready to be handstripped. The dog will be bathed after the coat has been stripped out.*

Above: *This is the finger and thumb method of handstripping, which some people prefer. Gently pluck the hair the way it grows.*

Right: *This clearly shows one half of the coat before stripping, the other after. Note the lovely rich colour of the stripped coat.*

Above: *The other method: hold the skin taut; push a little hair upwards and grasp between knife and thumb.*

Below: *While holding the tail with one hand, use your other finger and thumb to gently pluck away stray ends from the underside.*

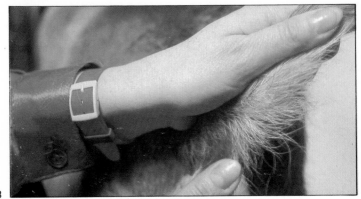

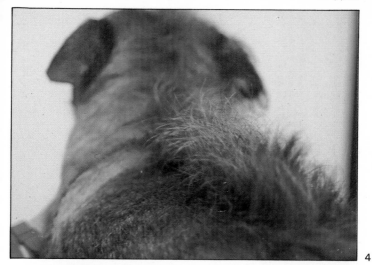

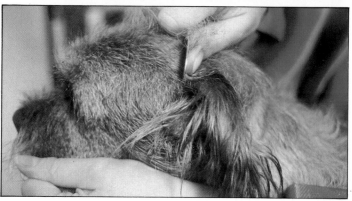

Above: *Gently strip out hair from the top of the head, cheeks and ears, leaving only the eyebrows and the moustache.*

Below: *Never allow the stripping knife to touch the dog's skin. Use your finger and thumb to pluck spiky hair from under the eyes.*

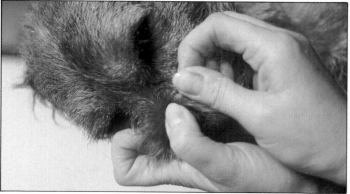

7

Above: *A rough grooming block can be used as shown to stroke the coat and achieve a smooth, glossy finish.*

Below: *Scissor away any wispy hairs from around the feet to give a neat effect, and down behind the backs of all four legs.*

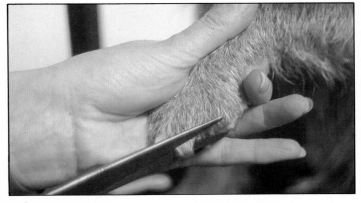

8

Below: *By lifting up the tail with one hand, use your free hand to scissor away any long, straggly hair from the hindquarters.*

Below right: *Handstripping, although time-consuming, can be rewarding when the result is such a smart, stylish little dog.*

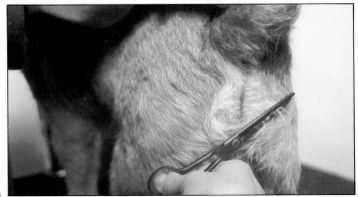

9

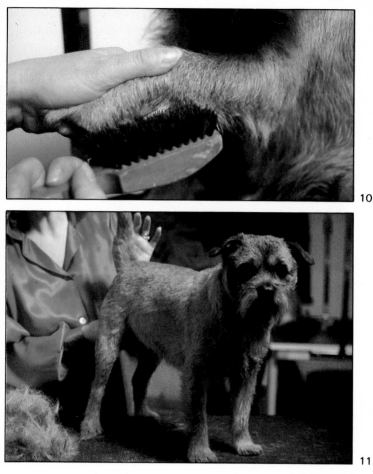

10

11

Top: *Gently brush your dog with a soft, natural brush to remove any dead hairs left behind from your handstripping of the coat.*

Above: *This little Terrier must feel much lighter and happier with all its dead hair removed – see the pile of hair on the left!*

12

Coat type: Spaniel/Handstrip

SPANIELS

English Cocker Spaniel

Style 1: Handstripped

Equipment:
Stripping knife (optional)
Slicker brush   Comb
Thinning scissors   Clippers
Clipper blade No 10   Grooming block (optional)

It is very important to aim for a natural look when handstripping your Spaniel. Thinning scissors are used to blend in the handstripped areas.

After stripping, attend to nails and ears, bathe (expressing anal glands, if necessary) and dry.

Grooming procedure
Body and legs Use a stripping knife or the finger and thumb

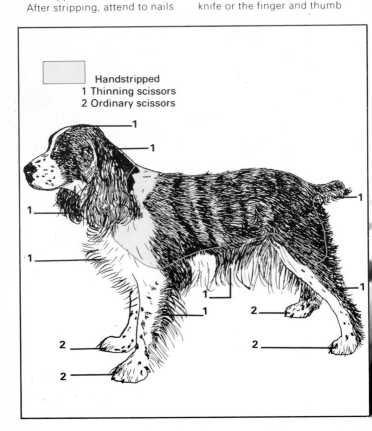

Handstripped
1 Thinning scissors
2 Ordinary scissors

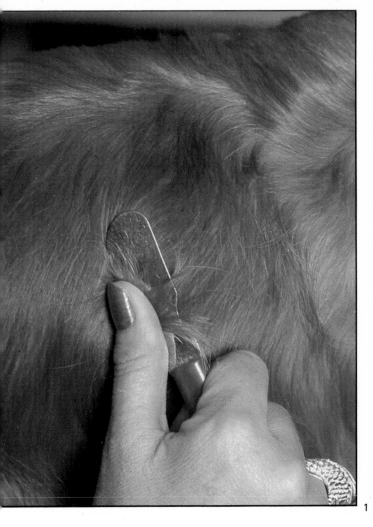

1

Above: *This Spaniel has a beautiful wavy coat. To maintain its natural look, use a stripping knife or finger and thumb to remove stray guard hairs.*

Left: *The diagram shows the area to be handstripped – use thinning scissors to blend with the longer feathering.*

method to strip the coat. The throat and neck areas can be thinned with thinning scissors, if desired. The underside of the tail is thinned and the feathering on

the legs combed out and thinned where necessary. Feathering on the front legs should be lightly thinned and tapered to the feet.

Feet Hold the feet towards you and brush the hair between the toes up and outwards. Holding the scissors parallel with the feet, trim away excess hair.

Head Use the thinning scissors to smooth the dome and blend the hair at the tops of the ears. Remove hair from the inside of the ears. Smooth over the head with a grooming block.

2

Above: *Use the edge of a No 10 clipper blade to clip out any matted hair from between the pads.*

Below: *If the hair is long and unruly on the throat and neck areas, you can use your thinning scissors to thin out the hair.*

3

Below: *The underside of the tail is also thinned, and comb out and thin the feathering on the legs where necessary.*

Right: *To achieve a glossy, smooth finish on the head, use a rough grooming block, while holding the head steady.*

4

Above: *Brush the hair between the toes up and outwards and trim hair with thinning scissors held parallel to foot.*

Below: *Use thinning scissors to smooth the dome and top portion of the ears. Clear hair from the inside of the ears.*

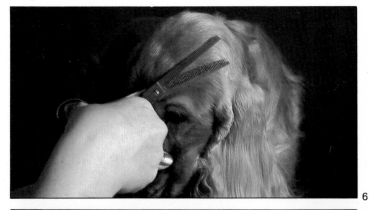

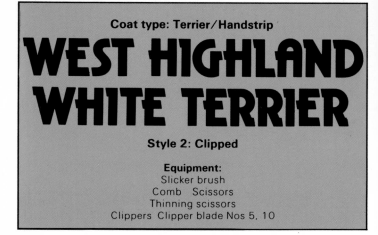

Coat type: Terrier/Handstrip

WEST HIGHLAND WHITE TERRIER

Style 2: Clipped

Equipment:
Slicker brush
Comb   Scissors
Thinning scissors
Clippers Clipper blade Nos 5, 10

As explained on pages 92-93 in connection with the Border Terrier, Terriers should, ideally, be handstripped. But this is not always possible – either because the texture of the coat does not suit the technique; the dog has a low tolerance level to having its hair plucked out; or you, as the owner, simply do not have enough time to devote to handstripping.

Grooming procedure
Go through the usual grooming preparation stages – cutting nails and cleaning ears; expressing glands, if necessary; bathing; cage or blow drying.

Below: *The diagram shows the clipped areas and direction of the clippers. Blend with thinning scissors for a natural look.*

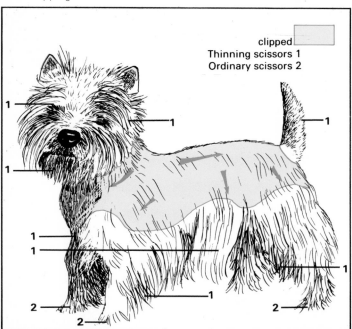

clipped
Thinning scissors 1
Ordinary scissors 2

Groin Clip the hair in this area with a No 10 blade.

Pads With the same blade, clip out any excess hair from under the pads.

Ears Clip the top half of the ear, both inside and out, using the No 10 blade.

Body Using the No 5 blade, start from behind the ears and clip down the entire back in a straight line, finishing about ½in (12mm) from the root of the tail. Go back to behind the ear and clip down and round the neck. Following the lie of the coat, clip the chest down to the breastbone. Clip down towards the ribs, gliding the clippers off the coat halfway down to leave the longer hair of the 'skirt'.

Blend the hair on the forechest into the body hair with thinning scissors (or ordinary scissors if you want your Westie quite short in coat). Neaten the skirt at the desired length using your scissors.

Legs and feet Scissor the hair around the feet to make them neat. Taper the leg feathering gradually down towards the feet. The legs should look straight.

Tail The tail should resemble an inverted carrot. Trim the hair short on the underside, tapering it towards the tip.

Head Never clip a Westie's head. Use ordinary scissors or thinning scissors (these give a more natural look to the head) to achieve a round, dish-like appearance. Comb the ruff outwards and forwards. Then round off both sides evenly with the scissors. Gently pluck any spiky, excess hairs from under the eyes using your finger and thumb. Comb the eyebrows forwards, and then trim them on a slant with thinning scissors.

Below: With all the preliminaries carried out – nail-cutting, bathing, drying etc, your Westie is ready for trimming.

1

Above: *Use a No 10 clipper blade to clip away the hair from the groin area, while holding the dog up behind its front legs.*

Below: *With the same blade, clip out any hair from between and under the pads; if left, this hair may form a mat.*

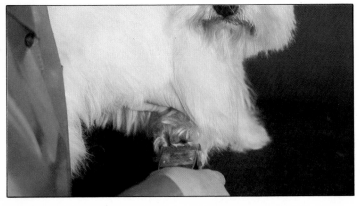

2

Below: *Still using the No 10 clipper blade, clip just the top half of the ears, both on the inside and outside as shown.*

Right: *The lie of the coat changes direction in this area, so follow it with the clippers. Clip down as far as the breastbone.*

3

Above: *Using a No 5 blade, start from behind the ears and clip down the entire back finishing about ½ in (12mm) from tail root.*

Below: *Go back to behind the ear and clip downwards and round the neck. Be careful to feed hair slowly through the blade.*

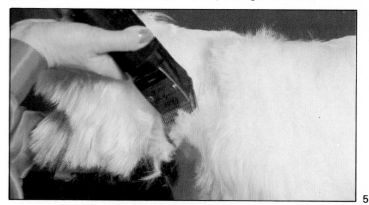

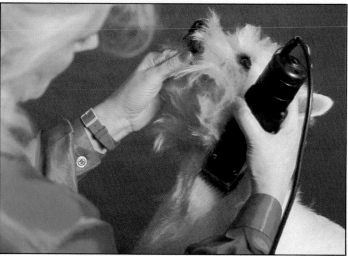

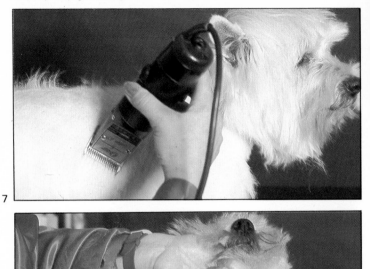

Top: *Clip down towards the ribs. Gradually lift off the clippers halfway down, so as to leave the skirt long – to be scissored later.*

Above: *Use thinning scissors to blend forechest hair with the clipped body hair. Use ordinary scissors for a shorter cut.*

10

Above: *Lifting each foot in turn, use your scissors to remove any excess hair from around the feet to give a neat, rounded edge.*

Below: *Taper the leg feathering to blend with the hair on the feet. If a very natural look is desired, use the thinning scissors.*

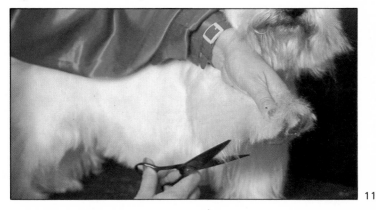

11

Below left: *Use your scissors to trim the skirt hair to whatever length you desire. Scissor to achieve a natural, straight look.*

Below: *Trim the hair on the underside of the tail quite short, leaving it wide at the base and tapering the hair towards the tip.*

12

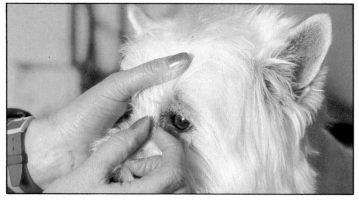

13

Above: *Using your finger and thumb, gently pluck away any unwanted spiky hair from the inner corners and under eyes.*

Below: *Work with your scissors from behind the ears, trimming the neck and head hair. Scissor downwards.*

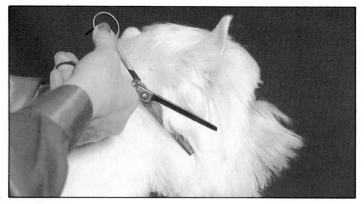

14

Below: *Never clip a Westie's head. All the work here is done with the scissors. Try to achieve a rounded effect.*

Right: *The finished West Highland White Terrier. The coat looks neat but natural; the dog does not look obviously clipped.*

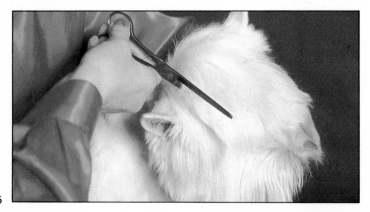

15

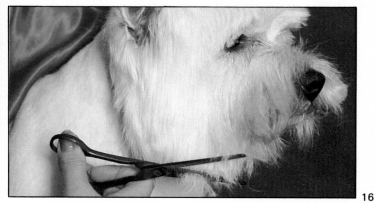

16

Above: *Hold the dog's head steady at the top and neaten the hair under the chin. Try for a crisp, rounded outline.*

Below: *Scissor the hair across the eyebrows using your thinning scissors for a soft effect. The Westie has a very appealing face.*

17

18

Coat type: Spaniel/Handstrip

SPANIELS

English Cocker Spaniel

Style 2: Clipped

Equipment:
Slicker brush
Comb   Scissors
Thinning scissors
Clippers
Clipper blade Nos 7f, 10

Many Spaniels have to be clipped because their coats are not suited to handstripping. The Spaniel illustrated here has a heavy coat. Many Spaniels with this type of coat have problems with hair matting between their toes, and the felting of the hair behind the ears. The ears of the Spaniel frequently attract burrs and grass seeds. It is essential to brush the heavily-coated Spaniel

daily to avoid such problems. If the ears become matted, follow the procedure recommended in Chapter Three for the Neglected Coat.

Grooming procedure
Follow the usual routine of cutting nails, cleaning ears, bathing and blow/hand drying. Clip out excess hair between the toes, as in the Handstrip style (page 100).

Groin Clip out this area using a No 10 blade.

Ears Using the same blade, clip the hair around the ear canal. Then clip the front and back of the ears about a third of the way down the ears.

Head Using the 7f blade, begin clipping from the base of the skull against the lie of the coat forwards towards the front of the head. Clip down the nose, over the muzzle and cheeks until the head and face are clean.

Body and legs With the No 7f blade, clip down the neck and shoulders with the lie of the coat (see diagram for clipper directions). Clip down as far as the breastbone. If the leg feathering is very thick, clip the front and side hair by gently skimming the clippers downwards but not over the feet.

Clip down the back and over the ribs without clipping the skirt featherings, and down the middle of the back legs leaving the front and back feathering.

Use your thinning scissors to thin out the featherings where needed. Above all, aim for a natural look.

Left: *This Spaniel's thick, woolly coat is best clipped after nail-trimming, bathing, blow-drying and clipping out feet.*

Below: *Area to be clipped and direction of clippers – use thinning scissors to blend with and thin out longer feathering.*

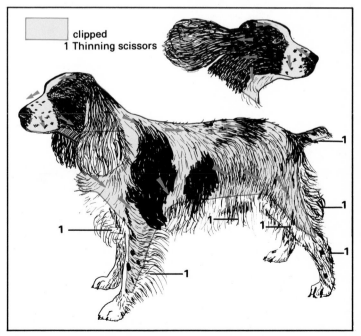

clipped
1 Thinning scissors

1

Above: *Using a No 10 clipper blade, hold the front of the Spaniel up so you can reach to carefully clip out the groin area.*

Below: *Using the same clipper blade, clip the hair away from around the ear canal while holding up the ear flaps.*

2

Below: *Still using the No 10 clipper blade, hold the ear outwards while you clip one-third of the way down the ear leather.*

Right: *Using a 7f blade, clip with the lie of the coat from now on, down the neck and shoulders. See diagram on page 111.*

3

4

Above: *Using a 7f blade, start by the base of the skull and gently clip against the lie of the coat, forwards over the head.*

Below: *Slowly clip down the nose, the sides of the muzzle, over the cheeks until the head and face are completely smooth.*

5

6

7

Above: *If the Spaniel has very woolly trousers, clip away the front and a little side hair, but stop before you get to the feet.*

Below: *Clip down the back, over the ribs and down the middle of the back legs, leaving skirt, back and front leg featherings intact.*

8

Below: *Start thinning all the feathering where necessary. The skirt should not slope upwards at the front.*

Right: *The finished Spaniel. The result is neat and natural. But scissor work like this does take time to perfect – so be patient!*

9

10

Above: *If there are any mats between the toes, brush hair up and outwards and thin. Hold scissors parallel to feet to trim.*

Below: *Use your thinning scissors to thin and trim the excess hair on the back legs from the hocks down, until it is flat.*

11

12

Appendix

USEFUL ADDRESSES
Kennel clubs
Australia Australian National Kennel Council, Royal Show Grounds, Ascot Vale, Victoria
Belgium Societe Royale Saint-Hubert, Avenue de l'Armee 25, B-1040, Brussels
Canada Canadian Kennel Club, 2150 Bloor Street West, Toronto M6S 1M8, Ontario
Caribbean The Caribbean Kennel Club, PO Box 737, Port of Spain, Trinidad
Denmark Dansk Kennelklub, Parkvej 1, Jersie Strand, 2680 Solrad Strand
Finland Suomen Kennelliitto-Finska Kennelklubben, Bulevardi 14A, Helsinki
France Societe Centrale Canine, 215 Rue St Denis, 75083 Paris, Cedex 02
Germany Verband für das Deutsche Hundewesen (VDH), Postfach 1390, 46 Dortmund
Holland Raad van Beheer op Kynologisch Gebied in Nederland, Emmalaan 16, Amsterdam, Z
Hong Kong Hong Kong Kennel Club, 3rd Floor, 28B Stanley Street, Hong Kong
India Kennel Club of India, 17 Mukathal St Purasawaltam, Madras 600 007
Ireland Irish Kennel Club, 23 Earlsfort Terrace, Dublin 2
Italy Ente Nazionale Della Cinofilia Italiana, Viale Premuda, 21 Milan
Malaysia Malaysian Kennel Association, No. 8, Jalan Tun Mohd Faud Dua, Taman Tun Dr Ismail, Kuala Lumpur
Malta Main Kennel Club, c/o Msida Youth Centre, 15 Rue d'Argens Str, Msida, Malta GC
Monaco Societe Canine de Monaco, Palais des Congrès, Avenue d'Ostende, Monte Carlo
New Zealand New Zealand Kennel Club, Private Bag, Porirua, New Zealand
Norway Norsk Kennelklub, Teglverksgt 8, Rodelokka, Postboks 6598, Oslo 5
Pakistan The Kennel Club of Pakistan, 17a Khayaban-I-Iqbal, Shalimar7, Islamabad
Portugal Cluba Portuguese de Canicultura, Praca D Joao da Camara 4-3°, Lisbon 2
Scotland The Scottish Kennel Club (the delegated Authority of the Kennel Club in Scotland) 6b Forres Street, Edinburgh, EH3 6BR
Singapore The Singapore Kennel Club, 170 Upper Bukit Timah Rd, 12.02 Singapore 2158
South Africa Kennel Union of Southern Africa, 6th Floor, Bree Castle, 68 Bree Street, Cape Town 8001, S Africa, PO Box 11280, Vlaeberg 8018
Spain Real Sociedad Central de Fomento de las Razas en Espana, Los Madrazo 20, Madrid 14
Sweden Svenska Kennelklubben, Norrbyvagan 30, Box 11043, 161 11 Bromma
Switzerland Schweizerische Kynologische Gesellschaft, Falkenplatz 11, 3012 Bern
United Kingdom The Kennel Club, 1 Clarges Street, London W1Y 8AB
United States of America American Kennel Club, 51 Madison Avenue, New York, NY 10010; The United Kennel Club Inc, 100 East Kilgore Road, Kalamazoo, MI 49001-5598

General
The United Kingdom
Battersea Dogs Home, 4 Battersea Park Road, Battersea, London SW8 4AA
The Blue Cross, Animal Hospital, 1 High Street, Victoria, London SW1V 1 QQ
British Small Animals Veterinary Association, 7 Mansfield Street, London W1M 0AT
British Veterinary Association, 7 Mansfield Street, London W1M 0AT
National Canine Defence League 1 Pratt Mews, London NW1 0AD
National Dog Owners' Association, 39–41 North Road, Islington, London N7 9DP
People's Dispensary for Sick Animals, PDSA House, South Street, Dorking, Surrey
Pet Food Manufacturers' Association 6 Catherine Street, London WC2B 5JJ
Pet Trade and Industry Association, 4th Floor, Onslow House, 60–66 Saffron Hill, London EC1N 8QX
The Royal Society for the Prevention of Cruelty to Animals, RSPCA Headquarters, Causeway, Horsham, Sussex RH12 1HG

The United States
American Animal Hospital Association, 3612 East Jefferson, South Bend, Indiana 46615
American Humane Association, (incorporating The Hearing Dog Association) 5351 Roslyn, Denver, Colorado 80201
American Society for the Prevention of Cruelty to Animals, 441 East 92nd Street, New York, New York 10028
American Veterinary Medical Association, 930 North Meacham Road, Schaumburg, Illinois 60196 °
Animal Welfare Institute, PO Box 3650, Washington D.C. 20007
The Fund for Animals, 140 West 57th Street, New York, New York 10019
Guide Dogs for the Blind, PO Box 1200, San Rafael, California 94902
The Humane Society of the United States, 2100 L Street, N.W., Washington D.C. 20037
International Association of Pet Cemeteries, 27 West 150 North Avenue, West Chicago, Illinois 60185
Leader Dogs for the Blind, 1039 South Rochester Road, Rochester, Michigan 48063
The National Dog Registry, 227 Stebbins Road, Carmel, New York 1051
Orthopaedic Foundation for Animals, 817 Virginia Avenue, Columbia, Missouri 65201
Owner Handler Association of America 583 Knoll Court, Seaford, New York 11783
Pet Food Institute, 1101 Connecticut Avenue N.W., Washington D.C. 20036
Rare Breeds Association, 31 Byram Bay Road, Hopatcong, New Jersey 07843
The Seeing Eye Inc, 100 East Kilgore Road, Kalamazoo, Michigan 49001

Grooming associations
The United Kingdom
Groomers Association, 4th Floor, Onslow House, 60–66 Saffron Hill, London EC1N 8QX

The United States
National Dog Groomers Association, PO Box 101, Clark, Pennsylvania 16113

MAGAZINES
General
The United Kingdom
The Kennel Gazette, 1 Clarges Street, Piccadilly, London W1Y 8AB
Dog World, 9 Tufton Street, Ashford, Kent TN23 1QN
Our Dogs, Oxford Road, Station Approach, Manchester
Dogs Monthly, Unit One Bowen Industrial Estate, Aberbargoed, Bargoed, Mid-Glamorgan, CF8 9ET

Pet trade
Pet Product Marketing, Bretton Court, Peterborough, PE3 8OZ
Pet Business World, 9 Tufton Street, Ashford, Kent TN23 1QN

Grooming
Grooming News, 4th Floor, Onslow House, 60–66 Saffron Hill, London EC1n 8QX

The United States
Pure-Bred Dogs, The American Kennel Club Gazette, 51 Madison Avenue, New York, New York 10010
Dog World, 300 West Adams Street, Chicago, IL 60606
Dog Fancy, P O Box 6050, Mission Viejo, CA 92690
Dogs USA (annual), P O Box 6050, Mission Viejo, CA 92690

Pet trade
Pet Age, 207 South Wabash Avenue, Chicago, IL 60604
Pet/Supplies/Marketing, 1 East First Street, Duluth, MN 55802
Pet Dealer, 567 Morris Avenue, Elizabeth, NJ 07208

Grooming
Groom and Board, 207 South Wabash Avenue, Chicago, IL 60604
Groomer to Groomer and *Groom-O-Groom*, Barkleigh Publications, 107 North Market Street, Mechanicsburg, PA 17055

Grooming suppliers
The United Kingdom
Diamond Edge Ltd, 126 Gloucester Road, Brighton, Sussex
Allbrooks Ltd, Wilton House, Lower Road, Chorleywood, Rickmansworth, Hertfordshire
Pets Paradise, 10 Tower Street, Kings Lynn, Norfolk

Petcetera etc, P O Box 112, Henley-in-Arden, Solihull, W Midlands
For shampoos and conditioners:
Phillips Yeast Products Ltd, Park Royal Road, London

Grooming tuition
Canine Comforts Ltd, 118 The Centre, Feltham, Middlesex
The author will occasionally train a student:
Dogroom, 44 Rutland Road, Hove, Sussex

Further Reading
The Stone Guide to Grooming For All Breeds, Ben and Pearl Stone, Howell Book House Inc, New York.
The All-Breed Dog Grooming Guide, Sam Kohl and Catherine Goldstein, Arco Publishing Inc, New York.
The Kalstone Guide To Grooming All Toy Dogs, Shirlee Kalstone, Howell Book House Inc, New York.
Dogs and How to Groom Them, Hilary Harmer
The Complete Poodle Clipping and Grooming Book, Shirlee Kalstone, Howell Book House Inc, New York.
A Standard Guide to Pure-Bred Dogs, H Glover, Macmillan London Ltd, London.
The American Kennel Club Official Publication, *The Complete Dog Book*, Howell Book House Inc, New York.
A Dog Of Your Own, Joan Palmer, Salamander Books Ltd, London.

GLOSSARY OF GROOMING TERMS

Apron: The long hair on the throat and below the neck on long-coated dogs.

Beard: The long hair that grows down from under the lower jaw.

Blow dry: Drying the coat with a hot-air dryer to straighten the hair while drying it, prior to trimming.

Bristle brush: A brush with tufts of soft, pure bristle, best for straight-silky haired breeds, eg the Yorkshire Terrier.

Cage dry: The dog is placed in a cage with a dryer attached, to dry the coat.

Clip: The method of trimming the coat in some breeds, eg Poodles and Terriers.

Dematting: Removing mats and tangles from a dog's coat.

Double Coat: An undercoat of soft, thick hair to warm the body, and an outer coat of coarse, strong hair to keep out dampness and cold.

Eyebrows: The arches of hair growing over the eyes, eg in Terriers.

Fall: Long hair over-hanging the face.

Feathering: Long, fine fringe of hair on the ears, legs, tail and body of breeds such as Spaniels.

Folds: Folds of flesh on the faces of certain hounds and other breeds.

Fringes: See *Feathering*.

Furnishings: The long hair on the front part of the head (ie the muzzle) of certain breeds.

Guard hairs: The longer, smoother, stiffer hairs that grow through the undercoat and normally conceal it.

Hand dry: See *Blow dry*.

Hand stripping: Removing the outer coat or dead hair using the finger and thumb or a stripping knife. See *Plucking*.

Harsh coat: A coarse or hard coat with a softer undercoat.

Leather: The flap of the ear.

Mats: Tangles in the coat.

Pin brush: An oval brush with a long handle, shaped like a human hair brush with rows of long metal pins. Best suited to long-haired breeds, eg the Afghan Hound.

Plucking: To pull out stray or dead hairs.

Pompon: A ball of hair left on the end of a Poodle's tail after clipping (as in the Lamb Clip).

Quick: The fleshy part of a dog's nail, containing nerves and blood supply.

Ruff: Thicker, longer hair growing around the neck.

Shedding: The natural loss of dead hair from the coat.

Slicker brush: A rectangular-shaped, flat-backed brush with short, bent-wire teeth set in a foam rubber pad. Recommended for use on curly coats, eg the Poodle.

Smooth coat: Short, sleek hair lying close to the skin.

Standard: The Standard of perfection for each breed.

Thinning scissors: Used for thinning out the coat. There are two types with either one serrated blade and one regular scissor blade, or two serrated blades.

Topknot: The longer, finer hair on the top of the head.

Towel dry: Drying smooth-coated dogs with a towel.

Trim: Grooming the coat by clipping or plucking.

Undercoat: The soft, furry wool beneath the outer hair of some breeds, giving protection against cold and wet.

Whiskers: The long hairs on the sides of the muzzle and under the lower jaw.

Wire-haired: Having a tough, dense, harsh coat.

Wrinkles: Loose folds of skin on the brows and sides of the face, eg in Bloodhounds, St Bernards, Pugs, etc.